The Walk with the Word
Psalm 119
Study Guide

(Small Group/Seminar Leader Edition)

"So faith comes from hearing,
and hearing by the word of Christ."
(Romans 10:17)

The Walk with the Word Psalm 119 Study Guide
(Small Group/Seminar Leader Edition)
By D. E. Isom
First Edition, August 2017

Scripture taken from the New American Standard Bible Copyright © 1960, 1962, 1963, 1968, 1971, 1972, 1973, 1975, 1977, 1995 by The Lockman Foundation. Used by Permission.
All other content, materials, etc. are Copyright © 2017 by Walk with the Word. Permission for personal and/or not-for-profit use freely granted. Any questions or comments should be directed to: Servant@WalkWithTheWord.org.

Walk with the Word
P.O. Box 9265
Redlands, CA 92375

Also available:
The Walk with the Word Psalm 119 Study Workbook
The Walk with the Word Psalm 119 Study Guide (Personal Edition)

ISBN: 978-1974478354

Contents

Preface 1
Study Preparations for Psalm 119 5
1 • Aleph (א): My Way is His Way (v.1-8) 13
2 • Beth (ב): Staying & Not Straying
(v.9-16) 14
3 • Gimel (ג): The Earthly vs. the Heavenly
(v.17-24) 16
4 • Daleth (ד): A Cure for the Blues
(v.25-32) 17
5 • He (ה): The Biblical Definition of
"Revival" (v.33-40) 18
6 • Vav (ו): The Cycle of the Word in the
Saved (v.41-48) 19
7 • Zayin (ז): Through It All (v.49-56) 20
8 • Heth (ח): My Portion (v.57-64) 21
9 • Teth (ט): The Right Result from
Discipline (v.65-72) 23
10 • Yodh (י): A Dual Working in Others
(v.73-80) 24
11 • Kaph (כ): When Will Justice Come?
(v.81-88) 25
12 • Lamedh (ל): Eternal Perfection
(v.89-96) 26
13 • Mem (מ): The Power of Meditation
(v.97-104) 27
14 • Nun (נ): The Light of the Word
(v.105-112) 29
15 • Samekh (ס): The Right Response
(v.113-120) 30
16 • Ayin (ע): I Am Your Servant
(v.121-128) 32
17 • Pe (פ): The Power of the Name
(v.129-136) 34
18 • Tsadhe (צ): The True Working of
Righteousness (v.137-144) 36
19 • Qoph (ק): In the Meantime
(v.145-152) 38
20 • Resh (ר): Revive Me (v.153-160) 40
21 • Shin (ש): Love for Your Word
(v.161-168) 42

22 • Tav (ת): The Word & Prayer
(v.169-176) 44
An Overall Look Back 47
Appendix "A": Psalm 119 Study Aids 53
Appendix "B": The Inductive Bible Study
Method 57
Appendix "C": Small Group Materials 65
   Psalm 119:1-8, 9-16, & 17-24 • Aleph,
      Beth & Gimel (#1-3) 67
   Psalm 119:25-32, 33-40, 41-48 • Daleth,
      He & Vav (#4-6) 74
   Psalm 119:49-56, 57-64, 65-72 • Zayin,
      Heth & Teth (#7-9) 80
   Psalm 119:73-80, 81-88, 89-96 • Yodh,
      Kaph & Lamedh (#10-12) 87
   Psalm 119:97-104, 105-112, 113-120 •
      Mem, Nun & Samekh (#13-15) 93
   Psalm 119:121-128, 129-136, 137-144 •
      Ayin, Pe & Tsadhe (#16-18) 100
   Psalm 119: 145-152, 153-160 • Qoph
      & Resh (#19-20) 110
   Psalm 119:161-168, 169-176 • Shin & Tav
      (#21-22) 117

Preface

> Thy word is a lamp unto my feet
> And a light unto my path.
> Thy word is a lamp unto my feet
> And a light unto my path
>
> When I feel afraid,
> And think I've lost my way,
> Still, you're there right beside me.
> Nothing will I fear
> As long as you are near,
> Please be near me to the end
>
> Thy word is a lamp unto my feet
> And a light unto my path.
> Thy word is a lamp unto my feet
> And a light unto my path
>
> I will not forget
> Your love for me and yet,
> My heart forever is wandering
> Jesus is my guide,
> And hold me to Your side,
> And I will love You to the end.

(Words and music © Warner/Chappell Music, Inc.)

Even if it cannot be remembered where it is precisely located in Scripture, it is probably safe to say that nearly every Christian can quote the 105th verse of Psalm 119, or at least hum this Amy Grant tune from which they remember it. However, like many of the "famous" verses ingrained in the common shared memory and culture of Western Christianity, because such have not been studied and understood within the whole biblical context in which they are found—in other words, the accompanying verses in the paragraph and sometimes the whole chapter surrounding them, we often end up only espousing **part** of the truth intended, or in some cases, missing the mark entirely. It is unrealistic not to expect that some, perhaps even many, will become quite agitated when it is pointed out that this song's lyrics are **not** actually biblical.

Although the song accurately quotes the King James Version of verse 105, nothing else in the accompanying verses can be found either in the whole of Psalm 119, nor the eight verse teaching which serves as its primary context. (Ps. 119:105-112) In fact, just do a quick comparison of the substance of each of the song's verses with the very next verse following 105 in the Psalm:

> *I have sworn and I will confirm it,*
> *That I will keep Your righteous ordinances.*
> *— Psalm 119:106*

Neither of the accompanying verses in the Grant rendition contain the kind of teaching you will find in the whole of Psalm 119, the source of her song's chorus and title. Those poetic additions essentially emphasize feeling near to Jesus, having Him close, and in the last line as a result of this feeling of proximity, loving Him. No, those are not bad or evil thoughts in and of themselves, but they do not reflect the true meaning of this Psalm dedicated to God's Word, which **actually** teaches, "When I feel afraid" I will obey God's Word **regardless** of my feelings and **in spite of** my fear. This Psalm does not make the request, "...hold me to Your side, and I will love You to the end", but rather that biblical love is proven by obedience to the whole of God's Word and ways to the very end in spite of circumstance, or any feeling, and even when we "feel" completely separated and alone from Christ. In fact, this Psalm actually teaches something more akin to, "I won't leave Your side regardless of what happens to me".

Preface

It may be subtle, but a truth has been lifted from Scripture and dressed up with mismatched accessories so that it is not fully teaching that which God's Word actually intended. **Nowhere** in this popular chorus is there even the notion, when it comes to God's Word, "*I have sworn it and I will confirm it*", much less "*keep*" it as is found in the following 106th verse, much less what is taught in all the rest of Psalm 119. Instead, a sense of nearness to Christ is substituted for a scriptural teaching on obedience *in spite of* one's feelings. An allusion more toward the nature of romantic love is mimicked rather than biblical love. This is actually not something trivial.

In its original context, this snippet of biblical text is about obedience to God's Word regardless of personal feelings, emotion or even in circumstances so overwhelming that we wonder if we will survive them. In the song, the crucial element of obedience experiences a substitution for a perceived feeling of closeness and further request to feel even closer. It undermines the basic biblical teaching of the true definition of "faith".

The real shame, however, is that every Christian is not intimately discipled in Psalm 119 to begin with, which as a whole turns out to be God's definitive explanation not just of how His overall given Word is organized, but how it is intended to work in the life of each believer. This will not be the last time the irony is observed that the largest chapter in all of God's Word is dedicated to explaining **God's Word**, and yet other than the one verse, it is rare that the mainstream believer knows anything else about it.

Even within most books dedicated to the subject of hermeneutics and associated overall approaches, this definitive word on the Word found within **the** Word is largely ignored. This is not to say that any or all of those approaches are wrong, but rather to suggest that they may not be the best starting point. Psalm 119 is not a whole, contained system in and of itself when it comes to God's Word, but it is, unquestionably, the foundational starting point. Everything else proceeds from here.

What follows is a complete inductive study on the whole of Psalm 119 which can be undertaken either personally or suitable for leading a small group or Sunday School class. "*Appendix 'A': Psalm 119 Study Aids*" provides a bookmark which can be printed and conveniently kept in one's Bible whenever studying Psalm 119, "*Appendix 'B': The Inductive Bible Study Method*" provides a review of the approach used at Walk with the Word (www.WalkWithTheWord.org) to produce this and all of its studies, and "*Appendix 'C': Handouts for Small Groups*" provides both a fill-in-the blanks handout for participants and a master key for small group leaders.

For further consideration, an 11 chapter book titled, "The Walk" is also available as a free download or online reading from the Walk with the Word website which is a discussion on how to incorporate God's Word into every area of ministry in any given congregation or fellowship. It is no coincidence that nearly all of its scriptural references come from Psalm 119.

Finally, it is important to keep in mind that this is not a teaching strictly limited to an Old Testament context, first of all because we know that Jesus **IS** "*the Word*" in its entirety (Jn. 1:1), and secondly because He confirms the same connection between believers and God's Word established through the Mosaic Law:

but showing lovingkindness to thousands, to those who love Me and keep My commandments. — Exodus 20:6

"He who has My commandments and keeps them is the one who loves Me; and he who loves Me will be loved by My Father, and I will love him and will disclose Myself to him." — John 14:21

Preface

How each believer approaches and handles the Word is actually a personal issue of love.

Notes on the Editions

This *Small Group Leader/Seminar Edition* contains all the materials to lead a small group or Sunday School class through 8-10 weeks/sessions covering the whole of Psalm 119. After going through each of the 22 parts of Psalm 119, this book contains an additional section which provides leader notes and group handouts consolidated into 8 consecutive lessons. The leader may want to additionally provide two introductory sessions using the material in *Appendix B: The Inductive Study Method* to familiarize students with its basic hermeneutical approach, and a second session drawing on *Study Preparations for Psalm 119* for the particular issues involved with Hebrew poetry.

Also included are a bookmark and handout which the leader can copy and provide to each participant. Many of these things are also available in color from the Walk with the Word website.

The Walk with the Word Psalm 119 Study Guide Workbook is designed for participants to take notes and annotate the NASB rendition of each section. This also has the benefit of keeping everyone on the same translation so as to minimize discussion about the various subtle differences in English renderings.

A *Personal Edition* of T*he Walk with the Word Psalm 119 study Guide* is also available in a smaller printed size (as well as a Kindle eBook) without all the accompanying small group materials and may be useful to be provided to each participant at the end of the series/seminar.

Study Preparations for Psalm 119

Each of these studies, as with all which are found on Walk with the Word (www.WalkWithTheWord.org), were created using the Inductive Bible Study (IBS) method. A basic review of this approach along with a handout on its fundamentals is provided in *"Appendix 'B'" The Inductive Bible Study Method*. This is why the overall format of each lesson comes in the form of questions which prod exploration and examination of the text. When employed in a teaching environment, the leader acts more as a facilitator by asking the questions and guiding the discussion so as to involve the participants in an exercise wherein they are being discipled to properly handle Scripture in parallel with self-examination. These studies are not intended to simply convey information as a result of the author's research or presentation, but for participants to actively seek and realize for themselves that which needs to be put into practice from God's Word.

Having first established the general approach being used, it is important to address some specific issues and parameters which we need to take into full consideration as we undertake our inductive study of Psalm 119 specifically.

Psalm 119 In History & As Literature

Many Bibles not only provide chapter and verse markings, but often include an annotation to show the beginning of each of five "books" (or scrolls) into which the 150 Psalms are divided. Some think this was a practical necessity because a single, giant scroll proved to be unwieldy and difficult to navigate, but many additionally assert that they were actually originally published as separate collections at different times. It appears that each of these five sections end with a Psalm which is also a benediction, so it seems that these five books were purposely collected and published together in some kind of organized fashion. (Although there is much academic debate concerning the particulars.)

If it seems strange that there are Psalms attributed to the authorship of David in all five portions published at different times in Israel's history, it is interesting to note that a prominent reference in one of the Dead Sea Scrolls (11QPs) ascribes to David the authorship of many thousands of psalms, which would mean there were far more than those captured in the canon of Scripture. This may not be so far-fetched when we consider that this is not unlike the scriptural statement that King Solomon *"also spoke 3,000 proverbs, and his songs were 1,005"*, (1 Ki. 4:32) which is another example where we know that Scripture records and documents far fewer of Solomon's works than he is acknowledged to have authored.

It would therefore appear there is plausible support that these collections of Psalms were not gathered and published all at once, but at different historical times. A common designation according to this school of thought is to attribute Book I to the time of King David, Book II to the time of King Solomon, Books III and IV to revivals under later kings of Judah such as Hezekiah or the like, and Book V to the school of Ezra after Israel's return from the Babylonian Captivity.

Although Psalm 119's author remains unknown, if such a timing holds true, this would place the general timeframe of its authorship at a very interesting time in Israel's history when they had finally ceased their pursuit of idolatry and become solely committed to God's Word. Israel in its return from the Captivity handled and pursued God's Word in a stark contrast to

Study Preparations

the reasons which led to the Captivity. At one point, during the Pre-Babylonian Captivity reign of Josiah, it appears that Israel had abandoned God's Word to such a great degree that they were down to a single copy. (2 Ki. 22:8-20)

An Acrostic Structure

From a literary standpoint, Psalm 119 is remarkable in many ways in that it is not only the largest of the all the chapters found in the Bible, but it is written in the style of acrostic Hebrew poetry. "Acrostic" means that each of its twenty-two eight verse stanzas begin with the next, successive letter in the Hebrew alphabet, starting with the first letter "*aleph*" and ending with the final "*tav*". (The Hebrew alphabet has fewer letters than English because it contains no vowels.) The use of an acrostic scheme was a tool for people of that language and culture to memorize the text and is not unique to Psalm 119 alone. Not only is this scheme employed in Psalms 9, 10, 25, 34, 37, 112 and 145, but is found in Proverbs 31:10-13, chapters 1-4 of Lamentations, and in Nahum 1:2-20.

In the area of Hebrew poetry, this was not simply a mnemonic device (a memorization aid), but was purposely used to convey the idea of order, progression, and completeness. Hence the added organization into groups of eight verses, "eight" being the biblical number for new beginnings. This is one of the primary functions of God's Word where both Testaments are concerned. When we come to faith in Christ, we now embrace and obey His Word, which guides us in the course of our own new beginning as a new creation in Him.

Hebrew Parallelism

The topic of Hebrew poetry is vast and also worthy of its own study, especially since it is obviously not composed according to a Western style of thinking or writing. A critical main feature which we have to keep in mind is that one of its primary characteristics is "parallelism"— that is, a technique which establishes a direct contrast or comparison of one thought with another. Modern Western writing rarely strays from a very straightforward organization of an introduction, a body of sequential points, and a summary conclusion, which Hebrew poetry, especially Psalms, rarely if ever follow. In order to bridge this gap between something originally written with a Middle Eastern mind and way of thinking and the modern reader's Western mindset, it takes some practice and accommodation to accomplish such. This is where the aforementioned Inductive approach greatly aids in making it relevant and understandable.

The Issue of Synonyms

It is important to clearly understand that unlike literature entirely created by human writers, the Holy Spirit-inspired Scriptures do not employ synonyms in the same way they do. In the course of most styles of literature, whether they be long like a novel or short like a poem or newspaper article, the repetitive use of the same word or phrase is perceived as bad writing and avoided even in the most casual of circumstances. Hence the more descriptive and creative synonyms which the writer can employ renders the reading more interesting, because use of the exact, same word over and over again seems to bore the reader, or at the least make it tedious and repetitive.

For instance, this would most certainly get a failing grade from the average English teacher:

> "My **really big** nose had a **really big** itch resulting in a **really big** sneeze which produced a **really big** booger."

The use of "really big" over and over again is not just boring, but approaches the definition of a literary crime by human standards. A much better grade would be obtained by using more colorful and creative synonyms in their place:

> "My **Pinocchio-sized** proboscis, with ever-increasing **seismic** rumblings, produced a **typhoon-class** ejection propelling a **capacious** booger into planetary orbit."

These are much more dramatic descriptions, but they all essentially mean the same thing—in this case, a variety of ways to creatively substitute alternatives for "really big" to keep the reader interested.

Similar But Different

Scripture does not employ synonyms in this manner, attempting to make the material more appealing or to retain the attention of the reader by providing alternating descriptions of the same thing. At its most fundamental core, God's Word is composed, word for word, of the absolute truth. Even though it was inspired to be written by more than forty writers spanning some 1,500 years or so, we can study the same word across them all and in every instance will find that each is consistent in its usage and does not vary; neither are there found to be synonyms employed in the same fashion as human-inspired literature. Just as God is eternal and unchanging, so is His Word.

For instance, the words "sin", "transgression" and "iniquity" are not describing the exact, same thing. The Holy Spirit did not determine that He had already used "sin", so now to keep us interested He would switch to "transgression" and then on to "iniquity". They all share some common characteristics, but in the end they are actually three different things. "Sin" is to fall short of the standard of God's Word, "transgression" is to rebel against the standard of God's Word, and "iniquity" is to twist or alter the standard of God's Word. Everyone can fall short in the case of "sin", but one cannot rebel without conscious awareness of the standard in the case of "transgression". And now we can see why "iniquity" as found throughout Scripture is assigned to the context of what those claiming a relationship with God are attempting to do to justify themselves. They are each used consistently throughout Scripture in connection to these specific conditions to teach about these three situations. They may all fall under the overall heading of what **we** generally label as "sin", but in their actual usage they are addressing **separate** issues.

These are actually unique and distinct words as offered in the original biblical languages and the reason why Bible translators select those specific English equivalents. ("*Chata'ah*" = "sin", Strong's #2401; "*pesha*" = "transgression", Strong's #6588; "*avon*" = "iniquity", Strong's #5771) We would be very upset to find out that they disregarded the original meanings and substituted one for another as if they were interchangeable synonyms, or even worse, threw in their own synonym of choice. (This is actually one of the hallmarks of a bad or corrupt translation.) They are merely translating the literal Hebrew word every time it is encountered, not choosing for themselves to employ an alternative to make the reading more interesting.

A Spiritual Emphasis

However, there **are** times when more than one description of the same person, place or thing is used within Scripture, but in such cases it not only falls short of being a true synonym in the secular literary sense, but actually provides tangible proof of Scripture being God-inspired and therefore set apart from all other literature.

Probably the most prolific example is when the nation is called "Israel" and at other times referred to as "Jacob". When they are called "Jacob", it is always in the context of the character of the original Patriarch Jacob, a representation of his old life as a deceiver and conniver; after his encounter with the Angel of the Lord, he comes away not only personally changed for the better, but renamed "Israel". "Jacob" is a picture of believers in their old, unsaved life, "Israel" a representation of their new life after coming to terms with Christ.

When God, through the Prophets, calls the nation "Jacob", He is referring to them in a backslidden condition in the character of the literal, unsaved figure, while "Israel" is employed when in the character of the right-standing person behaving in accordance with Jacob's change *after* his encounter with the Lord. They are not interchangeable synonyms even though they ultimately refer to the same thing, but are specifically selected to emphasize a different *spiritual* characteristic or condition.

Likewise we see this with other situations such as the use of "Zion" to describe the perfect heavenly counterpart to "Jerusalem" as the alternate downfallen earthly institution. They may both refer to the same city, but their use is consistently revealing these different spiritual perspectives so as to teach something greater. They are absolutely *not*, however, interchangeable synonyms for each other.

This is especially important to bear in mind when processing all the names Scripture gives for not only each member of the Godhead, but even for Satan and the Antichrist. Each of their many names represents a particular, personal characteristic or working which illuminates a key aspect of their overall nature and character. Many names are provided for each figure so we can construct a larger picture of who they are and how we should expect them to operate. Hence it is important to understand each of the meanings of "Satan", "Lucifer", "devil", and all others provided in Scripture because each is being used to convey specific information contributing to a much larger overall portrait; they are not simply used in random order to make the reading more interesting.

The Categories in Psalm 119

This long explanation is necessary because it pertains directly to any study of Psalm 119. When it is simply read instead of actually studied, it might appear that some Hebrew poet simply repeated a group of synonyms to make a very long poem on God's Word more interesting, or to fit his acrostic scheme. But in reality this Holy Spirit-inspired work, in the original language, is using eight distinct terms which our translators are faithfully rendering into the same, corresponding English equivalents so as to maintain the consistency and integrity of the text.

As it turns out, these eight terms are describing *different* spiritual aspects and purposes of God's overall Word, and these additionally act as the categories into which God's Word is actually organized. Together they combine into a greater portrait of God's *whole* Word. We are not just being given a lot of information as to their meaning in Psalm 119, but a host of examples from real life in order to understand how we can personally put them into practice. This is not simply a pursuit of knowledge or information, but one pertaining to our personal faithfulness.

There are many ways by which it is offered that the Bible is organized. This can be as simple as just "two testaments" to being more involved by associating each text with a type of literature or the chronology in which they were given, to name but a few of many, many proposed approaches. While such can be valuable tools in the course of our overall study, the foundation actually needs to start here.

Not surprisingly, the best explanation of how God's Word is fundamentally organized is offered by God's Word itself, and by providing it in the largest chapter of the 929 given in Scripture, it was meant to be noticed and taken seriously. It is a sad yet ironic commentary that so many Christians do not know what to do with God's Word when it is actually provided in the largest chapter of their Bible. The "manual" for our life actually itself came with a "manual".

All believers need to be acutely aware of these terms and their specific associated meanings in order to not only understand the exact context of each verse and stanza in Psalm 119, but so as to properly handle each of them whenever they are encountered in the rest of Scripture. Like all biblical terms which eschew the worldly use of synonyms, each is communicating a specific characteristic of an important aspect of God's given Word. How they are variously grouped and used in Psalm 119 specifically within each poetic stanza is actually teaching something much greater spiritually; how each is used throughout the whole of Scripture establishes not just a specific context for each of the passages within which they are found, but for their individual meaning overall.

This is a marvelous consistency which in and of itself testifies to the fact that the Bible cannot possibly be the invention of man, but divinely inspired across its many different authors, wide span of centuries, and from so many different backgrounds, locations and circumstances.

The eight terms provided in Psalm 119 as rendered by the New American Standard Bible (NASB) upon which all Walk with the Word studies are standardized are:

- "***Commandment***" (in Hebrew, "*mitsvah*"—Strong's #4687)

- "***Law***" (in Hebrew, "*torah*",--Strong's #8451)

- "***Ordinance***" or "***Judgment***" (in Hebrew, "*mishpat*"—Strong's #4941)

- "***Precept***" (in Hebrew, "*piqqud*"—Strong's #6490)

- "***Statute***" (in Hebrew, "*choq*" or "*chuqqah*"—Strong's #2706 & #2708)

- "***Testimony***" (in Hebrew, "*edah*" or "*eduth*"—Strong's #5713b & #5715)

- "***Way***" (in Hebrew, "*derek*" or "*orach*"—Strong's #1870 & #734)

- "***Word***" (in Hebrew, "*dabar*" or "*imrah*"—Strong's #1697 & #565a)

While they may enjoy shared, overlapping qualities overall, they are each ultimately describing a distinct component of what we generally refer to as "God's Word". Every verse in Scripture belongs to at least one of these categories; they may qualify for inclusion in more than one, but will always be found to belong to ***at least*** one.

There are those who are quick to point out that this list is incomplete because there is no category designated as "Prophecy". In reality, this is because the prophetic portions of God's Word do not belong to a separate category. When we carefully examine what is pronounced through one of God's Prophets, we find that the contents of what they are speaking belongs to one or more of ***these*** categories. One of the reasons there is so much confusion where the interpretation of the prophetic portions of God's Word are concerned is that they are unduly treated as separate and unique, something to be handled in a departure from the rest of His given Word. In fact, like the rest of God's Word, they are an integrated part of the whole and to be treated as such. Everything which a Prophet speaks actually belongs to one or more of these categories.

"Commandment" ("Mitsvah")

Used 22 times in Psalm 119, a "*commandment*" is what God has spoken which details the responsibilities of human beings when they live in a covenant relationship with Him. Especially in the Old Testament, commandments defined how Israel was to live in a covenant relationship with God, this being expounded upon in the New Testament.

It was the means of consecrating God's people to Himself. God specifically stated that those who *"keep My commandments"* are *"those who love Me"* (Ex. 20:6; Dt. 5:10), which Christ again reinforced in His teachings. (Jn. 14:15, 21, 23-24; 15:9-10) The Apostle John provided a particularly sharp assessment of this point:

> *By this we know that we have come to know Him, **if we keep His commandments**. The one who says, "I have come to know Him," and does not keep His commandments, is a liar, and the truth is not in him; but whoever keeps His word, in him the love of God has truly been perfected. By this we know that we are in Him: the one who says he abides in Him ought himself to walk in the same manner as He walked.* — 1 John 2:3–6

No covenant relationship can exist without putting into personal practice God's Word in this regard.

"Law" ("Torah")

Although the Pentateuch—the first five books of the Bible, are formally referred to as *"**The** Torah"*, the word *"torah"* itself generically means "teaching" or "instruction". Used 25 times in Psalm 119, God provides His instruction and personal teaching on how to live and serve Him. Some scholars make the distinction between the "ceremonial" law (the OT rites and ceremonies of worship), the "judicial" law (civil policy of the nation of Israel), and the "moral" law (God's binding of human conduct at all times). One of its primary functions is to personally instruct us so that we *"may not turn aside from the commandment, to the right or the left"*. (Dt. 17:18-19) This is but one example of how each of these categories share overlapping qualities and features, but ultimately describe a separate aspect of God's overall Word.

"Ordinance/Judgment" ("Mishpat")

Used 20 times, an *"ordinance"* or *"judgment"* is what we might call in modern times "case law". These are the verdicts, outcomes, or formal decrees established based on resolving a situation brought before the court. It describes the practical application of the Law in situations not specifically detailed word-for-word in Scripture so that we may understand how God's Word is applicable to every situation, and that it provides no loopholes. It describes a kind of third party presiding over the mediation of a dispute which may include decisions of approval as well as condemnation.

"Precept" ("Piqqud")

Used 21 times, a *"precept"* is a responsibility God has laid upon His people which is required **after** they have come into a personal relationship with Him. These are not things for which every person regardless of whether or not they are in a covenant relationship with God can automatically be held accountable; there are requirements for which God's people alone are responsible. Believers live according to a higher standard than the world's. The Hebrew word is derived from a word meaning "inspect".

"Statute" ("Choq", "Chuqqah")

Used 22 times, a *"statute"* is a prescribed task or boundary of a personal nature. These are things required such as limits or parameters for sacrifices, or the conditions for holy day observances, or the establishment of limiting guidelines such as who to marry, who to associate with, etc.

"Testimony" ("Edah", "Eduth")

Used 22 times, a *"testimony"* can be best thought of as "eye witness testimony". It is a powerful statement about the corroboration of the truth in all aspects of God's whole given

Word as provided by His personal witness of their detail, effects, and consequences.

"Way" ("Derek", "Orach")

Used 7 times, a *"way"* is derived from a Hebrew word specifically referring to a well-travelled path or road. It is a reference to human beings' actions which lead to staying on or straying from God's path, and is often contrasted with "my way". It is the course which God reveals as right in the character of Christ's disclosure, *"the way is broad that leads to destruction"* and *"the way is narrow that leads to life"*. (Mt. 7:13-14)

"Word" ("Dabar", "Imrah")

Used 18 times, the strict definition of these Hebrew terms for *"word"* describes a matter of cause spoken of directly by God. The dual use of *"dabar"* and *"imrah"* may be describing that what is spoken by God is continuously active whether spoken in general in the past or specifically to an individual in the present. The New Testament equivalent is the Greek *"logos"*.

Study Materials

In *"Appendix A: Psalm 119 Study Aids"*, a bookmark of these terms and a summary of their meaning is provided which can be printed and kept in your Bible as you study Psalm 119. Without understanding what each of these terms specifically refers to, it will not be possible to understand how and why they are being used by the psalmist in each individual instance, nor why they are uniquely grouped for each of the twenty-two lessons. Of course, all of the individual uses of each term can be isolated and grouped together, along with their usage in the rest of Scripture, in order to study and understand them in their own right, but there is still the original context in which they are presented in Psalm 119 which needs to be rightly understood as well. Why is a particular term used in that particular situation and/or in reference to that particular person or group? How is each category used to connect to the topic or object to which it is assigned? ***None*** of the usages are coincidental.

A Final Caveat

However, let's not make the mistake of solely approaching the study of Psalm 119 as a purely academic exercise. The issues of literary type, original languages and so forth certainly need to be taken into consideration, but we must never forget our primary goal is to apply God's Word to our life. In this case it can come across in a somewhat ironic fashion, because we are literally being instructed as to what needs to be done where God's Word is concerned *by* God's Word.

The psalmist is actually providing twenty-two teachings set in real life as examples of the working of Scripture, or at least how it ***should*** be allowed to work, on a very practical level. The examples and accompanying discussion are ***never*** theoretical, clinical, nor in any way some kind of distant academic conjecture. The purpose behind the whole collective Word of God is not solely limited to just information, instruction, nor even inspiration, but has as its ideal goal *incarnation*—that is, taking the Word of God to the level of the heart so as to result not only in changed living, but changed relationships. It is to become an actual part of us.

*All Scripture is inspired by God and profitable for **teaching**, for **reproof**, for **correction**, for **training in righteousness**; so that the man of God may be adequate, equipped for every good work.* — 2 Timothy 3:16–17

Notice that the common denominator in this list is nothing short of changed behavior not only according to our conduct with Christ personally, but in the course of our personal relationships.

The key to grasping incarnational reading is in understanding that the Bible is, in fact, the very words of God, relevant and applicable to the reader today. The reader "hears" God speaking through His Word because the reader puts it into practice, it changes him or her, and such become simultaneously more Christ-like both ***inwardly*** in their personal relationship with Him and ***outwardly*** in their personal relationships with others.

Psalm 119 is a special revelation in this regard, given to provide a direct guide as to what we are to actually ***do*** with God's Word. It is not a book to be kept an arm's length away, but Christ's working within to change us in our very heart, mind and soul so as to be visibly reflected in our treatment of and witness to others. That is, if we so allow it.

1 • Aleph (א): My Way is His Way (v.1-8)

Q: Who is "blessed"?
A: "...those...who walk in the law" (v.1) and "observe His testimonies" (v.2)—not just His instructions, but His affirming testimony of the benefits and requirements of His Word.

Q: Is this an unconditional state of blessedness?
A: It is experienced by those who are "*blameless*" only because of walking in, observing and seeking from the heart the pursuit of obedience to God's Word.

Q: How is the behavior of such a person visibly proven?
A: They "...*do no unrighteousness*" (v.3). Truly keeping God's Word is always reflected in the quality of one's behavior.

Q: Why are "statutes" connected with "commandments" in v.5-6?
A: The OT Covenant included commandments whose requirements could not be met without properly observing the rituals, observances and sacrifices detailed in God's Word. "*Commandments*" provide the requirement, "*statues*" specify how to carry it out.

Q: What is the personal effect when a believer does not keep His Word?
A: They experience shame (v.6) as His Word identifies their personal shortcomings in this regard.

Q: What is v.7 referring to?
A: The application of God's Word so as to be obedient in all things, properly applying God's Word even when a situation is not specifically spelled out word-for-word in Scripture.

Q: What is the potential result of a lack of obedience to His Word?
A: Being utterly forsaken. (v.8)

Application: *The way by which to walk "blameless" in Christ is to put into practice His ways as specified by His Word. This will not only be evident in our personal relationship with Him, but reflected in our visible behavior and witness to others*

Psalm 119:1-8

¹How blessed are those whose way is blameless,
Who walk in the law of the LORD.
²How blessed are those who observe His testimonies,
Who seek Him with all their heart.
³They also do no unrighteousness;
They walk in His ways.
⁴You have ordained Your precepts,
That we should keep them diligently.
⁵Oh that my ways may be established
To keep Your statutes!
⁶Then I shall not be ashamed
When I look upon all Your commandments.
⁷I shall give thanks to You with uprightness of heart,
When I learn Your righteous judgments.
⁸I shall keep Your statutes;
Do not forsake me utterly!

Simon

2 • Beth (ב): Staying & Not Straying (v.9-16)

Q: What is the main issue raised in v.9?
A: Keeping *"pure"*. This is the scriptural way of characterizing someone as being "unpolluted by sin". This can only be accomplished by not straying from God's Word. (Especially an issue for a *"young man"*.)

Q: How is this evidenced in the following verses?
A: The ability to *"not sin against You"* is only possible in someone who does not *"wander from Your commandments"* (v.10) and treasures God's Word *"in my heart"*. It describes someone who behaves and practices what is truly within them. (Jesus said in Mt. 15:17-20 it is what comes out of someone which proves his inner spiritual state.)

Q: What is the list of actions properly taken in v.9-13?

- *"Keeping"* (v.9)
- *"Sought"* (v.10)
- *"Treasured"* (v.11) / *highly*
- Testimony (*"I have told"*) (v.13)

We must be active both personally in our internal pursuit of a relationship with Christ, as well as externally as a visible example and testimony of the working of His Word to others through us.

Q: What is the contrast between v.10 & 14?
A: A true seeker from the heart does not confuse it with the earthly pursuit of material gain, which is one of the primary tools of sin.

Q: What is most likely listed as the greatest danger?
A: *"Do not let me wander"* (V.10) so as to avoid sin.

Psalm 119:9-16

⁹How can a young man keep his way pure?
By keeping it according to Your word.
¹⁰With all my heart I have sought You; *Stray*
Do not let me wander from Your commandments.
¹¹Your word I have treasured in my heart,
That I may not sin against You.
¹²Blessed are You, O LORD;
Teach me Your statutes.
¹³With my lips I have told of
All the ordinances of Your mouth.
¹⁴I have rejoiced in the way of Your testimonies,
As much as in all riches.
¹⁵I will meditate on Your precepts
And regard Your ways.
¹⁶I shall delight in Your statutes;
I shall not forget Your word.

Q: How is this followed up with a list of appropriate responses in v. 14-16?

- *"...rejoiced in...Your testimonies"* (v.14)—that is, the right response to God's affirmation of both the consequence and benefits associated with His Word.

- *"...meditate on Your precepts"* (v.15)—that is, obedience to those things for which believers are responsible after coming into a covenant relationship with God.

- *"...regard Your ways"* (v.15)—that is, seriously remaining on the path of God's Word.

- *"...delight in Your statutes"* (v.16)—that is, view positively the benefits of the boundaries and restrictions specified in God's Word.

- *"...not forget Your word"* (v.16)—that is, to bring to every decision, situation and relationship the application of God's Word for each and every thing.

Application: *Obedience to God's Word is the remedy for both wandering from God's path and preventing the allowance of the inevitable pollution of sin.*

3 • Gimel (ג): The Earthly vs. the Heavenly (v.17-24)

Q: Who are the people mentioned here? (Not every person has a proper name or stated position.)

- *"Your servant"* (v.17)
- *"a stranger in the earth"* (v.19)
- *"the arrogant"* (v.21)
- *"the cursed"* (v.21)
- *"princes"* (v.23)
- *"counselors"* (v.24)

> *Psalm 119:17-24*
>
> [17] Deal bountifully with Your servant, That I may live and keep Your word. [18] Open my eyes, that I may behold Wonderful things from Your law. [19] I am a stranger in the earth; Do not hide Your commandments from me. [20] My soul is crushed with longing After Your ordinances at all times. [21] You rebuke the arrogant, the cursed, Who wander from Your commandments. [22] Take away reproach and contempt from me, For I observe Your testimonies. [23] Even though princes sit and talk against me, Your servant meditates on Your statutes. [24] Your testimonies also are my delight; They are my counselors.

Q: How are these figures being compared and contrasted to each other?

> A: One who puts God's Word into practice is not only a *"servant"*—in the service of and indebted to the Master, but is *"a stranger on earth"*—that is, no longer a citizen of the earthly but rather the heavenly. They are no longer following the wisdom and advice of those still belonging to the earthly, who are here characterized as *"the arrogant"*, those who are ignorant of God's Word and ways, or even having a position of earthly authority such as *"princes"*.

Q: What do the earthly heap upon those focused on God's Word?

> A: *"...reproach and contempt..."* (v.22) This is to be the expected response from the earthly to those in obedience to God's Word.

Q: How does this situation highlight the believer's personal character trait, "My soul is crushed with longing after Your ordinances at all times"? (v.20)

> A: An ordinance is the application of God's Word in all things, particularly those which are not categorically spelled out word-for-word in the text of Scripture. It is erring on the side of God's Word where all things are concerned.

Application: *We should not be living as an earthly resident following its ways and listening to its messengers, but as "a stranger in the earth" who in all things regards God's Word as "my counselors".*

Simon 5/10/22 — Aiming to do 5 Stanzas tonight
— Looking at different translations has confused me!

Daleth

4 • Daleth (ד): A Cure for the Blues (v.25-32)

→ Do we ever feel them?

Q: How does the Psalm's author describe his personal condition?

1) • "My soul cleaves to the dust..." (v.25) — *or I am laid low in the dust*

2) • "My soul weeps because of grief..." (v.28) — *is weary with sorrow*

He is at a very low point both emotionally and spiritually.

Q: What is the good news regarding this according to v.26?
A: "I have told of my ways, and You have answered me". *recounted* He has received a response from the Lord.

Teach me your decrees.

Q: What is the nature of that response? Was it to perform a miracle or invoke divine intervention?
A: Encouragement to obey God's Word regardless.

Q: What are the keywords in v.25-29 which provide a basic structure of a prayer which God will always answer?

1) • "Revive me" (v.25) *or preserve my life.*
2) • "Teach me" (v.26) *your decrees/statutes*
3) • "Make me understand" (v.27) *the teaching of your precepts.*
4) • "Strengthen me" (v.28) *according to your word*
5) • "Remove the false way from me" (v.29) / *keep me from deceitful ways.*

Notice that these are all fulfilled by obedience and commitment to His Word, not by any kind of supernatural response.

Q: What is the primary benefit which is specified here for obedience to God's Word in spite of one's personal emotional state?
A: "For You will enlarge my heart". (v.32) *or You have set my heart free.*

Application: Obedience to God's Word and ways even when one is personally and emotionally low provides the appropriate remedy where it matters most: the heart.

Psalm 119:25-32 — *Peter*

I am laid low in the dust.
25 My soul cleaves to the dust;
Revive me according to Your word. — *preserve my life*
26 I have told of my ways, and You — *recounted*
have answered me;
Teach me Your statutes. — *decrees*
27 Make me understand the way of — *teaching*
Your precepts,
So I will meditate on Your wonders.
28 My soul weeps because of grief; — *is weary with sorrow*
Strengthen me according to Your
word.
29 Remove the false way from me, — *keep me from deceitful ways*
And graciously grant me Your law. — *be ... to me though*
30 I have chosen the faithful way; — *way of truth*
I have placed Your ordinances before — *set my heart on your laws*
me.
31 I cling to Your testimonies; O — *hold fast ... statutes*
LORD, do not put me to shame! — *let me be*
32 I shall run the way of Your — *in heart*
commandments,
For You will enlarge my heart. — *have set my heart free*

"GOD not only provides the rules and guidelines, but comes with us personally each day to strengthen us so that we can live according to those rules. All we must do is invite him and respond to his direction."

5 • He (ה): The Biblical Definition of "Revival" (v.33-40)

[handwritten top: "He" / "or Preserve in the NIV"]

Q: What are the related phrases in this passage which have in common the writer's desire for God's direction where His Word is concerned?

1) • (v.33) "Teach me" *to follow your decrees*
2) • (v.34) "Give me understanding" *& I will keep the law*
3) • (v.35) *Direct me in the path* "Make me walk in the path"
4) • (v.36) *Turn* "Incline my heart" *towards your statutes*
5) • (v.38) *Fulfill your promise* "Establish Your word to Your servant"

> **Psalm 119:33-40**
>
> ³³Teach me, O LORD, the way of *to follow your decrees*
> Your statutes,
> And I shall observe it to the end. *keep them*
> ³⁴Give me understanding, that I may *will*
> observe Your law
> And keep it with all my heart. *obey*
> ³⁵Make me walk in the path of Your
> commandments,
> For I delight in it. *there I find delight*
> ³⁶Incline my heart to Your *Turn*
> testimonies /statutes,
> And not to dishonest gain. *towards selfish*
> ³⁷Turn away my eyes from looking at *worthless*
> vanity, *things*
> And revive me in Your ways. *Preserve my life*
> ³⁸Establish Your word to Your *Fulfill your promise*
> servant,
> As that which produces reverence for *so that you may be feared*
> You.
> ³⁹Turn away my reproach which I *Take away the disgrace*
> dread,
> For Your ordinances are good. *laws*
> ⁴⁰Behold, I long for Your precepts; *how*
> Revive me through Your *Preserve in*
> righteousness.

Q: What are the desired results which reveal that this is not so much about knowledge as it is about faithfulness?

- (v.33) "...I shall observe it to the end." *will keep them*
- (v.34) "...that I may observe Your law..." *will keep*
- (v.34) "...that I may...keep it with all my heart." *and obey it with all my heart*
- (v.35) *for there I find delight,*
- (v.35) "...produces reverence for You."

Q: What are the potential pitfalls or obstacles that the writer desires to simultaneously overcome or avoid?

- (v.36) "Incline my heart...not to dishonest gain." *Turn not towards selfish*
- (v.37) "Turn away my eyes from looking at vanity..." *worthless things*
- (v.39) "Turn away reproach..." *Take away the disgrace* — *Shameful ways*

Point: Note how these items are issues of <u>pride</u> and the flesh which bring our attention down to <u>this present life</u> and <u>living for ourselves</u>, the diametric opposite of what takes place when we allow God's Word to take hold.

Q: What is probably the repeated keyword in these verses? What important definition is it providing within the overall context?

Preserve **A:** "Revive". (v.37, 40) The definition of a true "revival" is not the unsaved coming to the Lord, but the backslidden. *Preserve my life in your righteousness*

Application: Note how these combine to describe a lifestyle of putting God's Word into practice and not merely obtaining knowledge.

"Lord Don't let me make a mess of things" Read Rom 5:?? "overall"

Waw

6 • Vav (ו): The Cycle of the Word in the Saved (v.41-48)

Q: What is the dual nature of the working of God's Word where the believer is concerned in v.41-43?
A: In one's <u>personal</u> relationship with Christ it is grace and salvation, but where earthly relationships are concerned they are equally critical.

"for I have put hope in your laws"

Q: How would this relate to the statement, "For I will wait for Your ordinances" in v.43?
A: An <u>ordinance</u> is what we call "case law", the application of God's Word in situations which are not specifically, word-for-word addressed in Scripture. It is referring to a believer waiting for illumination from the Holy Spirit where God's Word is concerned in order to convey the right answer in terms of application of God's Word for a particular situation or person.

Q: What is the list of actions which characterize someone who, as specified in v.42, is biblically trusting in God's Word? *Translate*

What about you? How many do you do?

1. "I wait" (v.43) — *have put my hope*
2. "I will keep" (v.44) — *obey your law*
3. "I will walk" (v.45) — *about in freedom*
4. "I will also speak...and not be ashamed" (v.46) — *of your statutes & will not be put to shame*
5. "I shall delight" (v.47) — *in your Command*
6. "I shall lift up my hands" (v.48) — *to your commands*
7. "I will meditate" (v.48) — *on your decrees*

> **Psalm 119:41-48**
> ⁴¹May Your lovingkindnesses [unfailing love] also come to me, O LORD,
> Your salvation according to Your word; [promise]
> ⁴²So I will have an answer for him who reproaches me, [taunts]
> For I trust in Your word. [Do not snatch the word]
> ⁴³And do not take the word of truth utterly out of my mouth, [for I have put hope in your laws]
> For I wait for Your ordinances. [always obey]
> ⁴⁴So I will keep Your law continually,
> Forever and ever. [about in freedom]
> ⁴⁵And I will walk at liberty,
> For I seek Your precepts. [sought out] [statutes]
> ⁴⁶I will also speak of Your testimonies before kings
> And shall not be ashamed. [put to shame]
> ⁴⁷I shall delight in Your commandments, [commands]
> Which I love. [because I love them]
> ⁴⁸And I shall lift up my hands to Your commandments,
> Which I love;
> And I will meditate on Your statutes. [decrees]

Hazel

God's plan for our lives

Point: These provide a cycle covering not only our personal, private relationship with Christ, but our public testimony and witness of Him. At the heart of each one is an aspect of God's Word: "the word of truth", "Your law", "Your precepts", "Your testimonies", "Your commandments" (twice) and "Your statutes".

for I delight in your Commands because I love them

Q: What is significant about that which is repeated?
A: "Your commandments, which I love" (v.47, 48) is directly connected to the opening verse's identification of "lovingkindnesses" (OT term for grace) and "salvation". Biblical commandments are the requirements for a covenant relationship with God.

Application: The work of salvation can never be separated from the working of God's Word either within us personally or through us to others.

* *By living God's way we have freedom to fulfill God's plan for our lives*

The Psalmist talks about keeping the laws and yet being free. Contrary to what we often expect, obeying God's laws does not inhibit or restrain us. Instead it frees us to be what God designed us to be. By seeking God's salvation and forgiveness we have freedom from sin and the sensitive oppressive guilt.

7 • Zayin (ז): Through It All (v.49-56)

Q: What are the listed behaviors of those who reject God and His Word?

- (v.51) *"The arrogant utterly deride me..."*
- (v.53) *"Burning indignation has seized me because of the wicked, who forsake Your law."*

Point: *Because the unbelieving express contempt and ridicule for God's Word by forsaking it, they naturally render the same to those who cling to it.*

Q: Does this Psalm's author offer that this is something easily dealt with?

A: No, he specifically calls it *"my affliction"*. This is a Hebrew term which describes a state of hardship and trouble.

Q: What does the author do in order to deal with this hardship?

A: *"I...comfort myself"* (v.52) by...

- Remembering God's *"ordinances from old"* (v.52)—that is, the application of His Word in every situation, whether or not it is specifically articulated in Scripture, since the beginning. What He has done, He will continue to do—a continuous action.

- Making God's *"statutes...my songs in the house of my pilgrimage"* (v.54)—that is, remaining within the constraints of God's Word, recognizing we are just here temporarily.

- Remembering *"Your name in the night"* (v.55)—that is, obedient to God's Word and ways regardless of the hour or circumstance. The literal darkness of night is often a biblical metaphor for the worst of spiritual conditions.

Application: *Note that neither was a miracle sought to rescue the author personally, nor was God's imprecatory judgment called down to eliminate the source of the affliction. What he seeks is to maintain personal faithfulness to God's Word regardless.*

Psalm 119:49-56

⁴⁹Remember the word to Your servant,
In which You have made me hope.
⁵⁰This is my comfort in my affliction,
That Your word has revived me.
⁵¹The arrogant utterly deride me,
Yet I do not turn aside from Your law.
⁵²I have remembered Your ordinances from of old, O LORD,
And comfort myself.
⁵³Burning indignation has seized me because of the wicked,
Who forsake Your law.
⁵⁴Your statutes are my songs In the house of my pilgrimage.
⁵⁵O LORD, I remember Your name in the night,
And keep Your law.
⁵⁶This has become mine,
That I observe Your precepts.

8 • Heth (ח): My Portion (v.57-64)

Q: What is "portion" referring to? How does it provide an overall context?

A: This could easily be translated as "inheritance". It is used in Scripture to describe God's people...

> "For the LORD's portion is His people; Jacob is the allotment of His inheritance. (Dt. 32:9)

...and the land of Israel as a literal inheritance for His people...

> "Now therefore, apportion this land for an inheritance to the nine tribes and the half-tribe of Manasseh."(Josh. 13:7)

Likewise the believer's inheritance is not actually in the things of this world, but in the Lord as well, an indication of that we are children of the Father, not restricted to being physical descendants of life below.

> ... In Him also **we have obtained an inheritance**, having been predestined according to His purpose who works all things after the counsel of His will, to the end that we who were the first to hope in Christ would be to the praise of His glory. (Eph. 1:10a–12)

> Whatever you do, do your work heartily, as for the Lord rather than for men, knowing that **from the Lord you will receive the reward of the inheritance**. It is the Lord Christ whom you serve.(Col. 3:23–24)

> Blessed be the God and Father of our Lord Jesus Christ, who according to His great mercy has caused us to be born again to a living hope through the resurrection of Jesus Christ from the dead, **to obtain an inheritance which is imperishable and undefiled and will not fade away, reserved in heaven for you**, who are protected by the power of God through faith for a salvation ready to be revealed in the last time.(1 Pe. 1:3–5)

> **Psalm 119:57-64**
>
> 57 The LORD is my portion;
> I have promised to keep Your words.
> 58 I sought Your favor with all my heart;
> Be gracious to me according to Your word.
> 59 I considered my ways
> And turned my feet to Your testimonies.
> 60 I hastened and did not delay
> To keep Your commandments.
> 61 The cords of the wicked have encircled me,
> But I have not forgotten Your law.
> 62 At midnight I shall rise to give thanks to You
> Because of Your righteous ordinances.
> 63 I am a companion of all those who fear You,
> And of those who keep Your precepts.
> 64 The earth is full of Your lovingkindness, O LORD;
> Teach me Your statutes

Q According to v.58, what is the petitioner seeking for THIS life?

A: "...Be gracious to me according to Your word". In other words, he is not asking for supernatural intervention or God's judgment on those aligned against him, but to be treated correspondingly to his degree of faithfulness to God's Word.

Q: What are those things which bode well for the author in this regard where his personal relationship with God is concerned?

- (v.57) *"I have promised to keep Your words"*
- (v.58) *"I sought Your favor"*
- (v.59) *"I...turned my feet to Your testimonies"*
- (v.60) *"I...did not delay to keep Your commandments"*
- (v.61) *"I have not forgotten Your law"*

Q: And where his personal relationships are concerned?
A: *"I am a companion of those who fear You, and of those who keep Your precepts"*. (v.63) These are those who not only show the proper respect and reverence for God, but those who have entered into an actual covenant relationship with Him, since a precept can only be obeyed by a believer **AFTER** they have come to faith in God.

Q: What is here indicated that the author's endurance is an additional issue?
A: The reference in v.62 to rising and giving thanks at midnight, something often employed as a spiritual metaphor to speak of the intensity of spiritual issues or an overall spiritual environment.

Q: How do these verses end with a priority for believers where THIS life is concerned?
A: *"Teach me Your statutes"*—that is, the boundaries which God has set for believers designating requirements for them as to how to worship God and pursue biblical relationships, guidelines which allow us to live **IN** the world but **OF** the world..

***Application:** Believers devoted to God's Word understand that their "portion" or inheritance is not the things of this life, but the next, and always act accordingly in both their heavenly and earthly relationships.*

Les 12/10/22 — Be a doer. Looking forward
Things we can affect

9 • Teth (ט): The Right Result from Discipline (v.65-72)

Good to be afflicted.

Q: What is the present situation where the believer is concerned?

A: This is presented in the context of having experienced the discipline of the Lord, and effected the right response to it.

- (v.65) "You have dealt well with Your servant..." *Do good to*
- (v.67) "Before I was afflicted I went astray..." ✓
- (v.71) "It is good for me that I was afflicted..." ✓

Q: What was the right response to the Lord's discipline?

A: "...but now I keep Your word". (v.67) He is no longer just a "hearer" of the Word, but a doer. (Mt. 7:24-27; Ja. 1:23-25) *If you don't build your house on a rock*

Q: How is this believer's right response to God's Word contrasted to that of the unbeliever?

A: Not only are unbelievers' identified as "arrogant" and manipulating the truth (v.69)—the opposite of the working of God's Word, but the phrase, "Their heart is covered in fat" is an idiom used to describe someone who refuses to listen and change. *are callow & unfeeling*

Q: What are the requested action points now that the backslidden have properly responded to the Lord's discipline?

A: "Teach me good discernment and knowledge" (v.66) in *& Good judgement* combination with, "That I may learn". (v.71) It is far more valuable than anything which can be offered in this life, even a treasure of silver and gold. (v.72)

Application: Faithfulness is the only cure for unfaithfulness, and obedience *only are* for disobedience to God's Word and ways.

> *Psalm 119:65-72*
>
> ⁶⁵You have dealt well with Your servant,
> O Lord, according to Your word.
> ⁶⁶Teach me good discernment and knowledge,
> For I believe in Your commandments.
> ⁶⁷Before I was afflicted I went astray,
> But now I keep Your word.
> ⁶⁸You are good and do good;
> Teach me Your statutes.
> ⁶⁹The arrogant have forged a lie against me;
> With all my heart I will observe Your precepts.
> ⁷⁰Their heart is covered with fat,
> But I delight in Your law.
> ⁷¹It is good for me that I was afflicted,
> That I may learn Your statutes.
> ⁷²The law of Your mouth is better to me
> Than thousands of gold and silver pieces.

- Build your house on the rock
- Obey the word.
- ~~Teaching your decrees~~ Learn his decrees.
- Discipline yourself

10 • Yodh (י): A Dual Working in Others (v.73-80)

Q: According to v.73, for what purpose were we created?
   A: That we should obtain understanding through, and obedience to, God's Word.

Q: In the context of these verses, who are the main targets of a believer's obedience to God's Word?
   A: To other believers:

- *"those who fear You"* (v.74 & 79)
- *"those who know Your testimonies"* (v.79)

…and to non-believers:

- *"May the arrogant be ashamed"* (v.76)

Q: What are the attributes of God being emphasized in the course of being an example and witness to both believer and non-believer alike?
   A: *"Righteous"* (v.75), *"lovingkindness"* (v.76), and *"compassion"* (v.77). It is an equal application of truth and justice with grace and mercy.

Q: What is the stark difference presented in v.78?
   A: Whereas the unsaved *"subvert me with a lie"*, the response is to *"meditate on Your precepts"*, which are those things which only believers put into practice after coming into a personal relationship with God. In other words, the first reaction is not revenge, but self-examination, just as Jesus teaches. (Mt. 7:1-5)

Q: What is the proper result of such a self-examination?
   A: According to the closing verse, it is a blameless heart so to avoid the shame of misbehavior to either believers or unbelievers. One's witness remains intact.

> *Psalm 119:73-80*
>
> [73] Your hands made me and fashioned me;
> Give me understanding, that I may learn Your commandments.
> [74] May those who fear You see me and be glad,
> Because I wait for Your word.
> [75] I know, O LORD, that Your judgments are righteous,
> And that in faithfulness You have afflicted me.
> [76] O may Your lovingkindness comfort me,
> According to Your word to Your servant.
> [77] May Your compassion come to me that I may live,
> For Your law is my delight.
> [78] May the arrogant be ashamed, for they subvert me with a lie;
> But I shall meditate on Your precepts.
> [79] May those who fear You turn to me,
> Even those who know Your testimonies.
> [80] May my heart be blameless in Your statutes,
> So that I will not be ashamed.

Application: *There is a dual working of God's Word through us to build up others in the Body of Christ, and at the same time bear witness to those who have yet to accept Christ as their personal Savior. Our obedience to God's Word and ways simultaneously works on both.*

11 • Kaph (כ): When Will Justice Come? (v.81-88)

Q: What is this believer's spiritual condition according to v.81-82?
A: *"My soul languishes"* (v.81) and *"My eyes fail"*. (v.82)

Q: According to v.83, what is the source of this angst?
A: *"...those who persecute me"*.

Q: What, exactly, are they doing?
A: *"The arrogant have dug pits for me"* (v.85)—the way of describing in that time and culture traps being set.

Q: How do we know that this is speaking of traps of a spiritual nature?
A: Because in the same verse they are described as, *"Men who are not in accord with Your law"*, meaning they are operating outside and against it. This is further verified in v.86 when their persecution is identified in the form of *"a lie"*.

Q: Does the author ask for supernatural intervention or imprecatory judgment upon his persecutors?
A: Although *"They almost destroyed me on earth"*, (v.87) what is requested is be sustained as a faithful example of God's precepts—that which is required of believer's alone, and His testimony—both the consequences and benefits of His Word as stated by God personally.

Application: *Persecution of believers has always resulted in not just refining and strengthening the faith and walk of believer's, but in having a multiplying effectiveness where the opportunities to share the Gospel with unbelievers is concerned. There is unlimited time in eternity for justice, but only a short window in this life to avoid it.*

Psalm 119:81-88

[81]My soul languishes for Your salvation;
I wait for Your word.
[82]My eyes fail with longing for Your word,
While I say, "When will You comfort me?"
[83]Though I have become like a wineskin in the smoke,
I do not forget Your statutes.
[84]How many are the days of Your servant?
When will You execute judgment on those who persecute me?
[85]The arrogant have dug pits for me,
Men who are not in accord with Your law.
[86]All Your commandments are faithful;
They have persecuted me with a lie; help me!
[87]They almost destroyed me on earth,
But as for me, I did not forsake Your precepts.
[88]Revive me according to Your lovingkindness,
So that I may keep the testimony of Your mouth.

12 • Lamedh (ל): Eternal Perfection (v.89-96)

Q: What might be a very daunting contrast and comparison in these verses?
  A: The eternal faithfulness of God's Word extending both into eternity past and future (v.89-90) and our absolute dependence on it to first revive and sustain us.

Q: Why might the latter half of v.91 be telling us about an aspect of God's greater plan where we are concerned?
  A: The reference to, *"For all things are Your servants"* indicates that His intention for Creation is the same for us, that everything is created to ultimately worship and serve Him.

Q: Therefore, how does the believer personally proceed where God's Word is concerned?
  A: He commits to it in every conceivable way because *"Your word is settled in heaven"*, (v.89) whereas when it comes to the temporal things of this life, *"I have seen a limit to all perfection"*. (v.96)

Q: How does this contrast to both our personal nature's working on earth and that of unbelievers?
  A: Left to our own devices, we would perish in our affliction (v.92) having never recovered from it through God's Word (v.93), and if left up to *"the wicked"*—those willfully acting contrarily to God's Word and ways, they would destroy us.

Q: What is the closing verse describing?
  A: The Hebrew word *"broad"* is being contrasted with that of *"limit"*. It is a way of stating that earthly perfection is finite and can only extend so far, but God's Word is limitless.

Application: *In this life we have the choice of obedience to the eternal nature of God's Word, which not only established Creation and extends to eternity past, but to our eternity future, or remain with the limitations of earthly perfection, which is actually no perfection at all.*

Psalm 119:89-96

[89] Forever, O LORD,
Your word is settled in heaven.
[90] Your faithfulness continues
    throughout all generations;
You established the earth, and it
    stands.
[91] They stand this day according to
    Your ordinances,
For all things are Your servants.
[92] If Your law had not been my
    delight,
Then I would have perished in my
    affliction.
[93] I will never forget Your precepts,
For by them You have revived me.
[94] I am Yours, save me;
For I have sought Your precepts.
[95] The wicked wait for me to destroy
    me;
I shall diligently consider Your
    testimonies.
[96] I have seen a limit to all perfection;
Your commandment is exceedingly
    broad.

13 • Mem (מ): The Power of Meditation (v.97-104)

Q: What is the key action where our approach to God's Word is concerned, which is repeated twice in these verses?

A: *"Meditation"*. (v. 97, 99) It is incorporating God's Word into our prayer life so that they are inseparable.

Observation: *Scripture rarely advises us to simply "read" God's Word; the two most often used commands are to "study" and "meditate". This is because while prayer is the way WE talk to God, His Word is the way He most often talks to US. Without incorporating the Word in this way, prayer is a one-way conversation.*

Q: How would meditating on God's commandments (v.98) make one "wiser than my enemies"?

A: By definition a commandment is a requirement for someone who has entered into a covenant relationship with God. Therefore, by default, a believer's enemies are in a relationship with Satan, something which can be characterized even beyond just being unwise.

Q: How would meditating on God's testimonies (v.99) provide "more insight than all my teachers"?

A: By definition a testimony is God personally bearing witness to the benefits and/or consequences of obedience or disobedience where His Word is concerned. It is addressing the necessary issue that we pay more attention to God than man, even if our teachers are likewise believers.

> *Psalm 119:97-104*
>
> ⁹⁷O how I love Your law!
> It is my meditation all the day.
> ⁹⁸Your commandments make me wiser than my enemies,
> For they are ever mine.
> ⁹⁹I have more insight than all my teachers,
> For Your testimonies are my meditation.
> ¹⁰⁰I understand more than the aged,
> Because I have observed Your precepts.
> ¹⁰¹I have restrained my feet from every evil way,
> That I may keep Your word.
> ¹⁰²I have not turned aside from Your ordinances,
> For You Yourself have taught me.
> ¹⁰³How sweet are Your words to my taste!
> Yes, sweeter than honey to my mouth!
> ¹⁰⁴From Your precepts I get understanding;
> Therefore I hate every false way.

Q: How would meditating on God's precepts (v.100) provide understanding "more than the aged"?

A: By definition a precept is something required after a person enters into a covenant relationship with Christ. It is addressing the fervor with which one pursues their personal sanctification as it relates to obedience to His Word and ways, something a long-time believer has been engaged in longer than most. But even new believers can accelerate their growth by their obedience to His Word.

Q: How do v.101 & 102 describe additional requirements on our part where our personal behavior is concerned?

A: *"I have restrained my feet from every evil way"* is a proactive stance against personal sin, combined with doing so consistently as indicated by, *"I have not turned aside"*. It is avoiding part-time obedience to engage in full-time obedience.

Q: What might be a surprising benefit according to v.103?
   A: It is both enjoyable and refreshing to be in such a lifestyle.

Q: How does this ultimately change our attitude and behavior?
   A: Instead of entertaining the notion of, and sometimes pursuing, false ways, we come to hate them, and actively avoid them.

Application: *This all comports to the theme of meditating on God's Word, meaning that it is not just never out of our thoughts, but that we can no longer even entertain an alternative to first and foremost obey it.*

14 • Nun (נ): The Light of the Word (v.105-112)

Q: In the context of these verses, why is the lamp of God's Word so badly needed where the world is concerned?
  A: *"I am exceedingly afflicted"* (v.107) and *"The wicked have laid a snare for me"*. (v.110) In times of spiritual darkness, we are even more dependent on the light of God's Word to illuminate the sole path to which we need to cling.

Q: But how does v.109 identify an additional threat?
  A: *"My life is continually in my hand"* indicates freewill and choice, and the ever-present danger of making a personal decision contrary to God's Word and ways.

Q: How are "the wicked" trying to take advantage of this?
  A: By laying *"a snare"*, (v.110) something intended to take us away from the Lord. The remedy is to not go astray from God's Word, particularly in the case of His precepts, those things which are specifically required of a believer maintaining a right relationship with God.

Q: What is the believer's inheritance which matters in this life?
  A: *"Your testimonies forever"*. (v.111) For believers this is God's assurance of the benefits of obedience to His Word, and to the wicked the assurance of the consequences for disobedience.

> *Psalm 119:105-112*
>
> ¹⁰⁵Your word is a lamp to my feet
> And a light to my path.
> ¹⁰⁶I have sworn and I will confirm it,
> That I will keep Your righteous
>   ordinances.
> ¹⁰⁷I am exceedingly afflicted;
> Revive me, O Lord, according to
>   Your word.
> ¹⁰⁸O accept the freewill offerings of
>   my mouth, O Lord,
> And teach me Your ordinances.
> ¹⁰⁹My life is continually in my hand,
> Yet I do not forget Your law.
> ¹¹⁰The wicked have laid a snare for
>   me,
> Yet I have not gone astray from Your
>   precepts.
> ¹¹¹I have inherited Your testimonies
>   forever,
> For they are the joy of my heart.
> ¹¹²I have inclined my heart to
>   perform Your statutes
> Forever, even to the end.

Q: What is the kind of commitment to obedience which is required when it comes to God's Word?
  A: *"Forever, even to the end"*. (v.112) We are to never turn back.

Application: *God's Word will always provide enough illumination to allow us to keep to the proper path. As Jesus **IS** the Word, we can see why, in eternity, there is no need for any other Light.*

> *And the city has no need of the sun or of the moon to shine on it, for the glory of God has illumined it, and its lamp is the Lamb. — Revelation 21:23*

15 • Samekh (ס): The Right Response (v.113-120)

Q: What are the four types of non-believers identified and what do they all have in common?

A: They are the *"double-minded"* (v.113), *"evildoers"* (v.115), *"those who wander"*. (v.118), and *"the wicked"* (v.119) They are all different types of straying from God's Word.

- Someone who is *"double-minded"* cannot submit to God's law—His *"torah"* or instruction, because they vacillate between two or more opposing opinions.

    Elijah came near to all the people and said, "How long will you hesitate between two opinions? If the LORD is God, follow Him; but if Baal, follow him." But the people did not answer him a word. (1 Kings 18:21)

- An *"evildoer"* acts in direct contradiction to God's Word and ways and actively pursues an entirely opposite manner from God's Word.

- Someone who wanders is not making a commitment to anything, much less God.

- And the *"wicked"* are ultimately removed because they are the active agents of Satan and sin.

> *Psalm 119:113-120*
>
> [113] I hate those who are double-minded,
> But I love Your law.
> [114] You are my hiding place and my shield;
> I wait for Your word.
> [115] Depart from me, evildoers,
> That I may observe the commandments of my God.
> [116] Sustain me according to Your word, that I may live;
> And do not let me be ashamed of my hope.
> [117] Uphold me that I may be safe,
> That I may have regard for Your statutes continually.
> [118] You have rejected all those who wander from Your statutes,
> For their deceitfulness is useless.
> [119] You have removed all the wicked of the earth like dross;
> Therefore I love Your testimonies.
> [120] My flesh trembles for fear of You,
> And I am afraid of Your judgments.

Q: What is the most significant contrast between the believer and these types of non-believers as articulated in v.120?

A: The believer in **THIS** life fears God (*"my flesh trembles for fear of You"*), knowing from His *"case law"*(*"Your judgments"*) that there are no loopholes.

Observation: *It is interesting to note that in the Gospels, Jesus spends far more time and energy warning about hell than speaking about heaven.*

Q: While these various types of non-believers attempt their shenanigans, what is the appropriate response for the believer?

- (v.114) *"You are my hiding place"*
- (v.114) *"...and my shield"*
- (v.114) *"I wait for Your word"*

Application: *The right response to the total spectrum of non-believers is God's Word. It hides us, protects us, and always comes at the appropriate time.*

So will My word be which goes forth from My mouth;
It will not return to Me empty,
Without accomplishing what I desire,
And without succeeding in the matter for which I sent it. (Isaiah 55:11)

16 • Ayin (ע): I Am Your Servant (v.121-128)

Q: What is the nature of the situation being addressed?
A: Persecution or conflict being inflicted by others.

- (v.121) *"...Do not leave me to my oppressors."*
- (v.122) *"...Do not let the arrogant oppress me."*

Q: What are these oppressors specifically called? How does this reflect their attitude when it comes to God's Word?
A: They are called *"arrogant"* (v.122) and *"they have broken Your law"*. (v.126) They either think they know better, or above God's Word, or both.

Q: How does this serve as the basis for how the writer of this Psalm presents himself in contrast to the opposition's behavior?
A: He has a completely different regard and practice where God's Word is concerned:

- (v.122) *"My eyes fail with longing...for Your righteous word."*
- (v.127) *"...I love Your commandments..."*
- (v.128) *"I esteem right all Your precepts..."*
- (v.128) *"...I hate every false way."*

> *Psalm 119:121-128*
>
> ¹²¹I have done justice and righteousness;
> Do not leave me to my oppressors.
> ¹²²Be surety for Your servant for good;
> Do not let the arrogant oppress me.
> ¹²³My eyes fail with longing for Your salvation
> And for Your righteous word.
> ¹²⁴Deal with Your servant according to Your lovingkindness
> And teach me Your statutes.
> ¹²⁵I am Your servant; give me understanding,
> That I may know Your testimonies.
> ¹²⁶It is time for the LORD to act,
> For they have broken Your law.
> ¹²⁷Therefore I love Your commandments
> Above gold, yes, above fine gold.
> ¹²⁸Therefore I esteem right all Your precepts concerning everything,
> I hate every false way.

Application: *In other words, he is the opposite of someone characterized as arrogant and a law breaker in terms of his own personal treatment of God's Word. How would we fare in a similar comparison?*

Q: In the believer's statement of longing for salvation, what are the accompanying requests which work towards that goal?

- (v.124) *"...teach me Your statutes"*. These are limitations placed on believers for their own good. In this case, they stand in stark contrast to *"the arrogant"* (v.22) who *"have broken Your law"*. (v.126)

- (v.125) *"...give me understanding, that I may know Your testimonies"*. These are God's personal responses on the benefits and consequences of His Word and contrast the pursuit of *"every false way"* (v.128) which characterizes their overall behavior.

Application: *God's Word provides the believer insight not only into what God is doing in their personal life and situation, but into the root causes of those working in opposition to the believer. God's Word is a dual-edged sword cutting in opposite directions for each based on the condition of their heart, the believer for comfort and understanding, the non-believer for condemnation and judgment.*

Q: What might be interesting about the request, "It is time for the Lord to act"? What is the justification, and what specific actions are being requested?

A: The justification is, *"For they have broken Your law"* (v.126), but all of the requests have to do with requests for God to provide the believer a deeper understanding of the different aspects of His Word. There is never a request for something specific to happen to the non-believers, that being left solely to God's discretion.

Application: *Even when it comes to non-believers, the primary concern is still God's Word.*

Q: What are the labels presented in the course of these verses which best provide insight into the fundamental difference between the one following God's Word and ways versus the one who is not?

A: *"I am your servant"* (v.125) versus *"the arrogant"* (v.122). A Scripture-practicing believer is always first and foremost concerned about his own personal compliance with God's Word which results in a subservient relationship to Christ.

Application: *When a believer is actively opposed by others, the right response is to run back to God's Word. Even when completely justified by one's personal obedience so as to be the total innocent victim of oppression, it is not only left up to God to act according to His will, but seen as yet another opportunity to gain greater personal insight into His Word and ways.*

17 • Pe (פ): The Power of the Name (v.129-136)

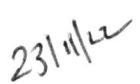

Q: What are the specific personal traits of someone who truly puts God's Word into practice?

- (v.131) *"I opened my mouth wide and panted, for I longed for Your commandments."* They do not merely view God's Word as leading to or describing life, but a vital integral part **OF** their life.

- (v.132) They *"love Your name"*—that is, their obedience stems from not simply following instructions, but motivated by personal love. An example is when David confessed, *"Against You, You only I have sinned"* (Ps. 51:4); where God's Word is concerned it is extremely personal.

- (v.136) *"My eyes shed streams of water, because they do not keep Your law."* Having personally established themselves in God's Word and ways, they experience an equally personal burden for those who have not.

Q: What is contained in v.132-135 which identifies the nature of what the writer is asking God to do where these qualities are concerned?

- (v.132) The writer begins by requesting treatment which begins with an examination of his own, personal faithfulness, and not for an exemption because of the lack of it.

- (v.133) This is a way of stating that the way to avoid sin's undue influence is by sticking to God's path alone. In NT terms we call this the process of "sanctification".

- (v.134) The writer does not request action against *"the oppression of man"* except that it go hand-in-hand with the opportunity, *"That I may keep Your precepts"*. It is an opportunity for personal witness where the working of God's Word is concerned.

- (v.135) The favor of God sought in this life is characterized as someone who is teachable when it comes to God's Word.

Psalm 119:129-136

129 Your testimonies are wonderful;
Therefore my soul observes them.
130 The unfolding of Your words gives light;
It gives understanding to the simple.
131 I opened my mouth wide and panted,
For I longed for Your commandments.
132 Turn to me and be gracious to me,
After Your manner with those who love Your name.
133 Establish my footsteps in Your word,
And do not let any iniquity have dominion over me.
134 Redeem me from the oppression of man,
That I may keep Your precepts.
135 Make Your face shine upon Your servant,
And teach me Your statutes.
136 My eyes shed streams of water,
Because they do not keep Your law.

Q: Why is it specified, "those who love Your name"? Why doesn't it state, "those who love You" to make it even more personal?

A: This is most likely another allusion to the importance of God's Word in the believer's life. A great many names for the members of the Godhead are provided in both Testaments, each provided in order to teach about important attributes. God is so vastly big, and yet His Word allows us to know Him personally through each of His names, teaching us what He is truly like. All of these attributes combine to teach about the inherent power in His name.

Application: *When we study in detail each of the names of God rather than just reading them, we not only acquire knowledge about His working and character, but it actually provides a foundation for why we love Him.*

Q: What is fundamentally different about Christ's name, for instance, from our own? How is it more than just a label?

A: The name of Christ actually has power and produces tangible results, unlike every other name which cannot result in anything.

> *Or do you not know that the unrighteous will not inherit the kingdom of God? Do not be deceived; neither fornicators, nor idolaters, nor adulterers, nor effeminate, nor homosexuals, nor thieves, nor the covetous, nor drunkards, nor revilers, nor swindlers, will inherit the kingdom of God. Such were some of you; but you were washed, but you were sanctified, but you were justified in the name of the Lord Jesus Christ and in the Spirit of our God. (1 Co. 6:9-11)*

Application: *A personal relationship characterized by biblical love with Christ is not just defined by our deep emotional and spiritual attachment to Christ personally, but it results in our deep concern for others who are not experiencing the same. We understand that it is not just the eternal consequences they will experience in the next life, but the benefits and blessings they are foregoing in this one.*

18 • Tsadhe (צ): The True Working of Righteousness (v.137-144)

Q: Based on its repeated usage in this passage, what is the main theme of this teaching?
A: *"Righteousness"*. (v.137, 138, 142, & 144) An additional related term is *"upright"*. (v.137)

Q: What are some of the accompanying descriptions of God's Word which go hand-in-hand with the quality of righteousness?

- (v.138) *"...exceeding faithfulness"*—that is, consistent in its adherence to God's Word and ways.

- (v.140) *"...very pure"*—that is, unpolluted by sin.

- (v.142) *"...an everlasting righteousness"*—that is, it is not temporal but stands from eternity past to eternity future.

Q: What are the personal issues which the writer provides insight, things with which he is struggling?
A: *"I am small and despised"* (v.141) and *"Trouble and anguish have come upon me"*. (v.143)

Q: But how does he deal with them?
A: *"...yet I do not forget Your precepts"* (v.141) and *"...yet Your commandments are my delight"*. (v.143) Regardless of the circumstances, he is still obedient to the biblical requirements for a covenant relationship with God (*"commandments"*) and God's requirements after such a commitment (*"precepts"*).

> *Psalm 119:137-144*
>
> [137] Righteous are You, O LORD,
> And upright are Your judgments.
> [138] You have commanded Your testimonies in righteousness
> And exceeding faithfulness.
> [139] My zeal has consumed me,
> Because my adversaries have forgotten Your words.
> [140] Your word is very pure,
> Therefore Your servant loves it.
> [141] I am small and despised,
> Yet I do not forget Your precepts.
> [142] Your righteousness is an everlasting righteousness,
> And Your law is truth.
> [143] Trouble and anguish have come upon me,
> Yet Your commandments are my delight.
> [144] Your testimonies are righteous forever;
> Give me understanding that I may live.

Application: When we find ourselves in similar situations, how often do we run to God's Word rather than put all our effort into praying a way out of the situation? Have you noticed how the words "prayer" and "pray" are seldom featured in Psalm 119? Why do you suppose that is? Consider the old saying, "Prayer is how we talk to God, His Word is how He answers us".

Q: How is this a major difference when it comes to those who follow His Word and those who do not?
A: *"My zeal has consumed me, because my adversaries have forgotten Your words"*. (v.139) It is the dual aspect that opponents disregard God's Word and live according to something else in its place, most often working and behaving in direct opposition, and in spite of what takes place; the practitioner, however, never steers away from obedience and compliance.

Q: What is probably the greater meaning in the closing request, "Give me understanding that I may live"?

A: The true biblical definition of "life" is to begin living now in accordance with God's Word and ways so that we may ensure eternal life; it is not to automatically seek comfort and security in the temporal years on this planet which is in general referred to as "life". Obedience to His Word allows us to live both now and in eternity to come.

__Application:__ No situation abrogates not just the requirements, but the greater personal need, for obedience to God's Word and ways. This is the working of righteousness where the believer is concerned.

Is there a verse that you have particularly liked from Psalm 119

Sis 7-12-22

19 • Qoph (ק): In the Meantime (v.145-152)

Q: In these opening verses, what is the list of actions which the writer has taken?

- (v.145) "I *cried* with all my heart, answer me, O LORD!" *call*
- (v.146) "I *cried* to You, save me..." *call out*
- (v.147) "I *rise before dawn and cry for help*..."

Q: What seems to be the cause of this angst?
A: "*Those who follow after wickedness draw near*". (v.150) It is not just an issue of dealing with those who may not believe, but those whose personal behavior and practices are completely opposed to those established by God's Word and ways, what is meant by their pursuing "*wickedness*".

Those who devise wicked schemes

Q: How would this relate to the assertion, "My eyes anticipate the night watches"? (v.148)
A: It is a way of stating that he has been looking for and waiting for an answer around the clock, not just temporarily engaged. It is a poetic way of describing both patience and endurance.

"My eyes stay open through the watches of the night"

Q: But in the meantime, what has been and continues to be his response?

- (v.145) "...I will observe Your *statutes*". *decrees*
- (v.146) "...I shall keep Your *testimonies*". *statutes*
- (v.147) "...I wait for Your *words*". *put my faith in your word*
- (v.148) "...I...meditate on Your *word*". *promises*

Q: In what context does the writer expect the response will come?

- (v.149) "*Hear my voice according to Your lovingkindness*". *in accordance with love* It is first and foremost a response rooted in God's grace and mercy.
- (v.149) "*Revive me, O Lord, according to Your ordinances*". *preserve my life* / *law* He will find that he has properly applied God's Word (the meaning of "*ordinances*") to his particular situation by remaining faithful to the Word through the entire situation, even while awaiting a final response.

Psalm 119:145-152

¹⁴⁵I cried with all my heart; answer me, O LORD! *call*
I will observe Your statutes. *decrees*
¹⁴⁶I cried to You; save me, *call out*
And I shall keep Your testimonies. *statutes*
¹⁴⁷I rise before dawn and cry for help;
I wait for Your words. *have put my hope in*
¹⁴⁸My eyes anticipate the night watches, *stay open*
That I may meditate on Your word. *promises*
¹⁴⁹Hear my voice according to Your lovingkindness; *love*
Revive me, O LORD, according to Your ordinances. *preserving my life* / *laws* *devise wicked schemes*
¹⁵⁰Those who follow after wickedness draw near;
They are far from Your law.
¹⁵¹You are near, O LORD,
And all Your commandments are truth. *true*
¹⁵²Of old I have known from Your testimonies *statutes*
That You have founded them forever. *to last forever*

Long ago I learned from your statutes

- (v.152) *"Of old I have known from Your testimonies that You have founded them [Your commandments] forever."* Faith in the foundation of God's Word serves to justify our need for His Word to be equally enforced in the present circumstances.

Q: What might be ironic about the statement in v.150? How does it contrast to the writer's own situation?

A: Because of non-compliance with God's Word, the wicked are *"far from Your law"*. But while in this case the petitioner feels his own distance from God, he is actually drawn close because of consistent faithfulness to His Word even in the absence of a definitive resolution by earthly standards. In spiritual things as well as earthly, appearances can be deceiving.

Application: *What is the correct response to every earthly situation where God's Word is concerned? Trust in God's Word.*

Call out to God.

20 • Resh (ר): Revive Me (v.153-160)

Q: What is the repeated request which provides the overall context? How is this to be accomplished?

- (v.154) "...Revive me according to Your word". *[preserve my life / promise]*
- (v.156) "...Revive me according to Your ordinances". *[preserve my life / laws]*
- (v.159) "...Revive me, O LORD, according to Your lovingkindness" as resulting from, 'Consider how I love Your precepts". *[preserve my life]*

Application: *When seeking a personal revival or restoration, these are probably the three most important aspects of God's Word—"Your word", "Your ordinances" and "Your precepts", because they are not revisiting the basic requirements of a covenant relationship, but addressing the deeper aspects which come after. They are foundational to a continuing and deepening relationship, whereas "commandments" and "law" are the entry level requirements. We have already "entered" once, the issue is now returning to what we already know and continuing in faithfulness to what subsequently follows.*

Q: What is requested as part of the overall process to be revived?

- (v.153) "Look upon my affliction and rescue me..." *[suffering / save, deliver]*
- (v.154) "Plead my cause and redeem me..." *[Defend]*

The request is for Christ our Advocate to *"rescue"* and *"redeem"* *[deliver]*, terms Scripture often associates with salvation.

> *"Even now, behold, my witness is in heaven,*
> *And my advocate is on high. — Job 16:19*

> *My little children, I am writing these things to you so that you may not sin. And if anyone sins, we have an Advocate with the Father, Jesus Christ the righteous; and He Himself is the propitiation for our sins; and not for ours only, but also for those of the whole world. — 1 John 2:1–2*

Psalm 119:153-160

¹⁵³Look upon my affliction and rescue me,
For I do not forget Your law.
¹⁵⁴Plead my cause and redeem me;
Revive me according to Your word.
¹⁵⁵Salvation is far from the wicked,
For they do not seek Your statutes.
¹⁵⁶Great are Your mercies, O LORD;
Revive me according to Your ordinances.
¹⁵⁷Many are my persecutors and my adversaries,
Yet I do not turn aside from Your testimonies. *[faithless]*
¹⁵⁸I behold the treacherous and loathe them,
Because they do not keep Your word.
¹⁵⁹Consider how I love Your precepts;
Revive me, O LORD, according to Your lovingkindness.
¹⁶⁰The sum of Your word is truth,
And every one of Your righteous ordinances is everlasting.

Q: Is there an indication in the text of how salvation relates to both the righteous and the wicked?
   A: *"Salvation is far from the wicked, for they do not seek Your statutes"*. (v.155) Obedience to God's Word and ways is directly connected to both.

Q: Is a source for his "affliction" (v.153) and need for the Lord to "Plead my cause" (v.154) provided?
   A: In v.157 they are specifically identified as *"my persecutors and my adversaries"*. They are coming from earthly antagonists.

[handwritten: my foes who persecute me]

Q: In this situation, how does he personally respond while awaiting God's resolution to these things?
   A: *"...Yet I do not turn aside from Your testimonies"*. (v.157) In spite of the circumstances, the chief response is to faithfully keep God's Word.

[handwritten: not turned ... statutes]

Q: : Why is this especially a difficult thing to do?
   A: *"I behold the treacherous and loathe them, because they do not keep Your word"*. (v.158) They are not only refusing to adhere to the same standard where God's Word is concerned, but they engage in the perversion of their own word by means of perpetrating treachery, a Hebrew word which is closely aligned with the meaning of deceit. (Hebrew *"mirmah"*, Strong's #4820)

[handwritten: Do we loathe people who are faithless?]

Q: How does the concluding thought contrast to the treachery of the wicked?
   A: *"The sum of Your word is truth"* accepts God's Word as absolute even in spite of the personal circumstances, and *"...every one of Your righteous ordinances is everlasting"* is a way of stating that in spite of the temporal situation, the result is unalterably permanent when in compliance with God's Word.

Application: While we are free to express our feelings, it cannot be automatically assumed that God will answer by altering or changing our emotions, which are subject to unpredictable shifts when His Word is not. As with most things in life, it is not a test of our feelings but a test of faith, especially when it comes to trusting God's already provided Word.

[handwritten notes:]

Favourite Verse

v 103 How sweet are your words to my taste
105 Your Word is a lamp to my feet & a light for my path

v 28 ? Songs
v 37 Worthless
v 51 Being mocked
v 64 Your love
v 72 Precious to ~
v 76

130

21 • Shin (ש): Love for Your Word (v.161-168)

Q: How might the issue, "Princes persecute me without cause" (v.161) be associated to something relevant that we might experience in our own life?
  A: This is easily substituted for governmental persecution and/or harassment.

Q: But like all the other types of opposition identified in Psalm 119 as originating with various types of human antagonists, how is the response still exactly the same as previously and repeatedly rendered?
  A: *"...but my heart stands in awe of Your words"* (v.161) is exactly in line with every reaction to persecution, opposition and unfair treatment, to remain steadfast in obedience to God's Word and ways regardless.

Q: What is the main thought being conveyed where God's Word in general is concerned?
  A: It is not just admiration for the Word or obedience out of fear, but a genuine love for it.

- (v.161) *"...my heart stands in awe of Your words."*
- (v.163) *"...I love Your law."*
- (v.167) *"...I love them [Your testimonies] exceedingly."*

> *Psalm 119:161-168*
>
> ¹⁶¹Princes persecute me without cause,
> But my heart stands in awe of Your words.
> ¹⁶²I rejoice at Your word,
> As one who finds great spoil.
> ¹⁶³I hate and despise falsehood,
> But I love Your law.
> ¹⁶⁴Seven times a day I praise You,
> Because of Your righteous ordinances.
> ¹⁶⁵Those who love Your law have great peace,
> And nothing causes them to stumble.
> ¹⁶⁶I hope for Your salvation, O Lord,
> And do Your commandments.
> ¹⁶⁷My soul keeps Your testimonies,
> And I love them exceedingly.
> ¹⁶⁸I keep Your precepts and Your testimonies,
> For all my ways are before You.

Q: And what is the chief benefit listed of this deeper relationship with God's Word?
  A: *"Those who love Your law have great peace, and nothing causes them to stumble"*. (v.165)

Application: *It is not peace as the world defines it which obedience to God's Word and ways engenders, but the peace which comes to a believers who is living sin-free and in perfect character with His Word, what is here referred to as not stumbling.*

Q: What are the proper actions to be taken which are listed in v.166-168 undertaken by believers concerning God's Word?

- (v.166) *"I...do Your commandments."*
- (v.167) *"My soul keeps Your testimonies..."*
- (v.168) *"I keep Your precepts and Your testimonies..."*

Application: *How well do we recognize that biblical obedience is love-based? When we have an authentic relationship where we truly love someone, we have no issues of submission or compliance because incorporation of the rules is simply a pleasant part of that experience. We willfully limit our behavior.*

Q: What is significant about the closing confession, "For all my ways are before You"?
  A: It is recognition that nothing is hidden from Christ.

Q: How does this fit in with the overall experience of love for His Word?
  A: It is the conscience realization that there is no fear of everything being an open book to Christ when we are walking in accordance to His Word. His ways become our ways.

Application: *We need to recognize that our personal love for Christ must go hand-in-hand with our acknowledgment of the Apostle John's foundational teaching that Christ Himself is "the Word". (Jn. 1:1-5) We cannot love one with the other, which means not merely reading or listening to the Word, but becoming "an effectual doer". (Ja. 1:25) There is no authentic love relationship with Christ in the absence of complete obedience to His Word.*

> *"You shall not worship them or serve them; for I, the L*ORD *your God, am a jealous God, visiting the iniquity of the fathers on the children, on the third and the fourth generations of those who hate Me, but showing lovingkindness to thousands,* **to those who love Me and keep My commandments***. — Exodus 20:5–6*
>
> *"****If you love Me, you will keep My commandments****. — John 14:15*
>
> *"****If you keep My commandments, you will abide in My love****; just as I have kept My Father's commandments and abide in His love. — John 15:10*

22 • Tav (ת): The Word & Prayer (v.169-176)

Q: Why might this closing section be surprising where the activity of prayer is concerned?
  A: Although in each of the 22 instances the writer is obviously engaging in prayer, he rarely addresses the subject directly as provided here.

Q: Why do you suppose that is?
  A: Because true, biblical faith is first and foremost grounded in obedience to God's Word and ways, for which no amount of prayer can act as a substitute.

Point: *A common false teaching is that "faith" is believing in something hard enough that God is moved to materialize it, especially in the areas of personal finances, health and worldly comfort. It is a false faith which is more akin to blowing out the candles on a birthday cake and wishing really hard for a pony. Biblically speaking, where there is no obedience to God's Word, for the believer there can be no authentic faith.*

> *So faith comes from hearing, and hearing by the word of Christ. (Romans 10:17)*

Q: What are the aspects of prayer which are presented here? And what is the requested response to each action?

> ### Psalm 119:169-176
>
> ¹⁶⁹Let my cry come before You, O LORD;
> Give me understanding according to Your word.
> ¹⁷⁰Let my supplication come before You;
> Deliver me according to Your word.
> ¹⁷¹Let my lips utter praise,
> For You teach me Your statutes.
> ¹⁷²Let my tongue sing of Your word,
> For all Your commandments are righteousness.
> ¹⁷³Let Your hand be ready to help me,
> For I have chosen Your precepts.
> ¹⁷⁴I long for Your salvation, O LORD,
> And Your law is my delight.
> ¹⁷⁵Let my soul live that it may praise You,
> And let Your ordinances help me.
> ¹⁷⁶I have gone astray like a lost sheep; seek Your servant,
> For I do not forget Your commandments.

- (v.169) *"Let my cry come before You..."* This is not a cry of desperation, but the Hebrew expression of rejoicing or making a joyful noise. The expected response is, *"Give me understanding according to Your word."*

- (v.170) *"Let my supplication come before You..."* A *"supplication"* is usually a request for mercy for oneself or others in the form of a prayer. The expected response is, *"Deliver me according to Your word."*

- v.171) *"Let my lips utter praise..."* Biblical praise is completely devoted to the elevation of the character and working of God and completely devoid of any aspect of our self. The expected response is, *"...teach me Your statutes."*

- (v.172) *"Let my tongue sing of Your word..."* This is describing one's testimony, not just making music. There is no expected response, but rather further personal affirmation, *"For all Your commandments are righteous."*

Point: *Notice how this is not some kind of "wish list" for something material or of benefit in this world, but approaching God in affirmation and praise of what His Word works in us.*

Application: *Because we most often employ prayer when things are wrong due to our own disobedience to God's Word, it is consumed with pleas for some kind of divine remedy. In this example, going to the Lord in a condition of obedience results in an overwhelming attitude of praise and thanksgiving.*

Q: What is the actual list of requested actions being submitted?

- (v.173) *"Let Your hand be ready to help me…"*
- (v.175) *"Let my soul live that it may praise You…"*
- (v.176) *"…seek Your servant…"*

Q: What is the reciprocal response on behalf of the believer for these things?

- (v.173) *"…I have chosen Your precepts."*
- (v.174) *"…Your law is my delight."*
- (v.175) *"…let Your ordinances help me."*
- (v.176) *"…I do not forget Your commandments."*

Application: *A prayer life which fails to not merely incorporate God's Word, but falls short of seeking an even greater personal commitment to it, is at best marginal. Such reveals both a wrong set of priorities and a shortfall where pursuing a deeper relationship where Christ is concerned.*

An Overall Look Back

Psalm 119 does not simply begin and end with designating the categories which fundamentally shape the whole counsel of God's Word, but as has been seen over the course of these studies, the seeming repetition is actually accompanying ***instruction*** as to what, exactly, we are ***to do*** with every aspect of God's Word. It is an exhaustive coverage of not just the requirement but the ***need*** to put God's Word and ways into practice.

It is an interesting shared behavior among Christians that when faced with almost any personal issue, dilemma or point of contention, our knee-jerk reaction is to go to the Lord in prayer. Psalm 119 is certainly written in the form of a prayer, but it rarely addressed that action on its own. This is because just engaging in prayer alone is an incomplete action where God is concerned; it is achieved by an equal pursuit of God's Word. In fact, this is the human side of that conversation which is devoted to making a personal accounting of what is personally being accomplished where God's Word is concerned. As it has been famously stated, "Prayer is the way we talk to God, but Scripture is the way He talks back to us". But it is very difficult to sincerely study this Psalm without realizing how little we incorporate God's Word as the key part of any issue's resolution. Far too often we stare into the great expanse waiting for some kind of cosmic, divine response when it is already residing in that Book on our desk we seem to rarely open, but won't go to church without.

Persecution & Opposition

One of the most prolific, repeated items is how to properly respond to our mistreatment at the hands of others, and in particular, opposition aimed squarely at our faith. Just look at the following examples, and take special note of the remedy common to each case:

*Even though **princes sit and talk against me**,*
Your servant meditates on Your statutes. (Ps. 119:23)

May Your lovingkindnesses also come to me, O L<small>ORD</small>,
Your salvation according to Your word;
*So I will have an answer for **him who reproaches me**,*
For I trust in Your word. (Ps. 119:41-42)

The arrogant utterly deride me,
Yet I do not turn aside from Your law.
I have remembered Your ordinances from of old, O L<small>ORD</small>,
And comfort myself. (Ps. 119:51-52)

*The cords of **the wicked have encircled me**,*
But I have not forgotten Your law. (Ps. 119:61)

The arrogant have forged a lie against me;
With all my heart I will observe Your precepts. (Ps. 119:69)

*May **the arrogant** be ashamed, for they subvert me with a lie;*
But I shall meditate on Your precepts. (Ps. 119:78)

An Overall Look Back

__The arrogant have dug pits for me__,
Men who are not in accord with Your law.
All Your commandments are faithful;
They have persecuted me with a lie; help me!
They almost destroyed me on earth,
But as for me, I did not forsake Your precepts. (Ps. 119:85-87)

__The wicked wait for me to destroy me__;
I shall diligently consider Your testimonies. (Ps. 119:95)

Your commandments make me wiser than __my enemies__,
For they are ever mine. (Ps. 119:98)

__The wicked have laid a snare for me__,
Yet I have not gone astray from Your precepts. (Ps. 119:110)

Depart from me, __evildoers__,
That I may observe the commandments of my God. (Ps. 119:115)

Redeem me from __the oppression of man__,
That I may keep Your precepts. (Ps. 119:134)

Many are __my persecutors__ and __my adversaries__,
Yet I do not turn aside from Your testimonies. (Ps. 119:157)

__Princes persecute me without cause__,
But my heart stands in awe of Your words. (Ps. 119:161)

In such situations, are we inclined to run to God's Word and ensure our own, personal compliance? How well do we recognize that the spiritual goals behind these actions from protagonists across the board is to first and foremost affirm our personal obedience to God's Word and ways? That is how they invoke a response from us that is most often unloving, un-Christian, and just plain unbiblical. If we stick to acting and behaving in strict accordance with God's Word, we will *always* find ourselves on the right path to providing a godly, biblical response empowered by the Holy Spirit rather than resorting to our old, fleshly desire for self-satisfaction.

In Numbers 22-24 is the important story of how the king of Moab tried to purchase the aid of a professional prophet to bring a spiritual and literal downfall upon the advancing Israelites, a teaching referred to in the New Testament as well by Peter (2 Pe. 2:10b-16), Jude (Jude 1:10-12) and Christ (Rev. 2:14). Essentially, as long as Israel was in compliance with God's Word, this effort was unsuccessful. However, what turned things around is revealed in Scripture by the disclosure that by the *"counsel of Balaam"*, Israel was seduced to *"trespass against the LORD"*. (Num. 31:16) When they abandoned their faithfulness to God's Word and ways, their greatest problem was not actually the enemy's intentions and even actions brought against them, but the corruption of their personal relationship with God. As with all the situations offered in Psalm 119, and corroborated by parallel scriptural passages and accounts, the best knee-jerk reaction we can have is to run to God's Word and ensure that we are obedient regardless. The remedy is *always* first and foremost faithfulness to His Word.

Trials, Tribulation & Endurance

Likewise, when undergoing personal tests and trials, it is not prayer alone which proves the quality of our faith, but the degree to which we are obedient to His Word:

An Overall Look Back

*Remember the word to Your servant,
In which You have made me hope.*
This is my comfort in my affliction,
That Your word has revived me. (Ps. 119:49-50)

*My eyes fail with longing for Your word,
While I say, "When will You comfort me?"
Though I have become like a wineskin in the smoke,*
I do not forget Your statutes. *(Ps. 119:82-83)*

*If Your law had not been my delight,
Then* ***I would have perished in my affliction.*** *(Ps. 119:92)*

I am exceedingly afflicted;
Revive me, O LORD, according to Your word. (Ps. 119:107)

*Look upon my affliction and rescue me,
For I do not forget Your law.
Plead my cause and redeem me;*
Revive me according to Your word. *(Ps. 119:153-154)*

It is actually the primary action we are to undertake in the pursuit of the oft-encountered related biblical theme of endurance:

*O LORD, I remember Your name in the night,
And keep Your law. (Ps. 119:55)*

*At midnight I shall rise to give thanks to You
Because of Your righteous ordinances. (Ps. 119:62)*

*My life is continually in my hand,
Yet I do not forget Your law. (Ps. 119:109)*

*I am small and despised,
Yet I do not forget Your precepts. (Ps. 119:141)*

*I rise before dawn and cry for help;
I wait for Your words.
My eyes anticipate the night watches,
That I may meditate on Your word. (Ps. 119: 147-148)*

How often do we pray for encouragement and the ability to endure without simultaneously consulting God's Word? By failing to do so, we are foregoing the comfort of God's response as it is revealed through His written Word, which in turn strengthens our resolve to remain obedient regardless of our personal feelings or the most overwhelming nature of the circumstances. Again, it is through His Word by which we most often hear His reassurances.

Additional Issues

The practice of always first returning to God's Word is at the heart of nearly every Christian behavior and situation. It the right response to the Lord's discipline...

*Before I was afflicted I went astray,
But now I keep Your word. (Ps. 119:67)*

*It is good for me that I was afflicted,
That I may learn Your statutes.
The law of Your mouth is better to me
Than thousands of gold and silver pieces. (Ps. 119:71-72)*

It is the right response to abstaining from sin...

An Overall Look Back

I have restrained my feet from every evil way,
That I may keep Your word.
I have not turned aside from Your ordinances,
For You Yourself have taught me.
How sweet are Your words to my taste!
Yes, sweeter than honey to my mouth!
From Your precepts I get understanding;
Therefore I hate every false way. (Ps. 119:101-104)

It is the right response to extreme emotional anguish...

My soul weeps because of grief;
Strengthen me according to Your word. (Ps. 119:28)

It is the right response on which to base our proper approach of God...

Establish Your word to Your servant,
As that which produces reverence for You. (Ps. 119:38)

It is the right response of our personal praise...

Seven times a day I praise You,
Because of Your righteous ordinances. (Ps. 119:164)

It is the foundation for our personal ministry to the Body of Christ...

I am a companion of all those who fear You,
And of those who keep Your precepts. (Ps.119:63)

May those who fear You turn to me,
Even those who know Your testimonies. (Ps. 119:79)

It is the foundation for our attitude when it comes to our consideration of the unsaved...

My eyes shed streams of water,
Because they do not keep Your law. (Ps. 199:136)

And yes, it is foundational to our prayer life...

Let my cry come before You, O LORD;
Give me understanding according to Your word.
Let my supplication come before You;
Deliver me according to Your word. (Ps. 119:169-170)

The repeated point within Psalm 119 is how a believer, in **every** situation, runs as fast as they can to God's Word, not just to read it, but for the purpose of self-examination. In every scenario, to what degree am I sure that I am first and foremost in compliance with God's Word?

Christians so often pursue activities and courses of action which contain **some** elements of spirituality without full incorporation of God's Word. We have seen how a popular song can be accepted within the Church because it was never formed nor subsequently evaluated against the standard of God's Word. But this happens in very broad strokes in many ministries, movements and relationships.

Simply reading Scripture every day is not enough; it has to become seamlessly integral with every part of our Holy Spirit-filled lives. Without doing so, it is like a deaf person who is still able to talk out loud to someone, but incapable of hearing the response. Likewise are all things for a Christian without the fundamental incorporation of God's Word, with the primary goal of a personal checklist to be obedient regardless.

Many wonder what is wrong with our times, especially **within** the Church proper, but it is respectfully submitted that *this* is what actually needs to be addressed more than anything else where Christians are concerned. A proper return to and implementation of God's Word resolves every issue of sin, false teaching, and ill behavior. The lack of it is why "Christ" so often cannot be seen within a "***Christ***"ian.

So faith comes from hearing, and hearing by the word of Christ. (Rom. 10:17)

Appendix "A": Psalm 119 Study Aids

What follows is a bookmark which can be copied and provided to study participants. This is designed to be kept in one's Bible as a quick reminder of the definition of each of the eight categories Psalm 119, and Scripture as a whole, use to describe God's Word. Following this page with a single bookmark, when just a single instance is needed, is a page with four copies. If desired, color versions of these are available as a free download from the Walk with the Word website. (www.WalkWithTheWord.org)

Appendix "A": Psalm 119 Study Aids

Psalm 119	Commandment ("Mitsvah") Used 22 Times	Law ("Torah") Used 25 Times	Ordinance/ Judgment ("Mishpat") Used 20 Times	Precept ("Piqqud") Used 21 Times	Statute ("Choq"/ "Chuqqah") Used 22 Times	Testimony ("Edah"/ "Eduth") Used 25 Times	Ways ("Derek"/ "Orach") Used 7 Times	Word ("Dabar"/ "Imrah") Used 25 Times
There are 8 different words used throughout Psalm 119 to describe God's Word. Make sure of their definition each time they are used, & the correct context in which they are employed. These are **NOT** synonyms with the same meaning, but each communicate something very specific.								
	Requirements for living in a covenant relationship with God.	"Torah" is not only the name of the Law, but also means "teaching" or "instruction".	What we might call "case law", the application of God's Word in situations not specifically addressed in Scripture word-for-word.	From Hebrew word for "inspect". The requirements of God's people AFTER entering into a covenant relationship with Him.	Prescribed tasks and boundaries of a permanent nature, such as rules for holy days, sacrifices, limits on marriage, etc.	"Eye witness" testimony. God's personal corroboration of the benefits and/or consequences where His Word is concerned.	Refers to a well-traveled road. The course which God reveals as right & which humans stick to or stray from.	A matter or cause spoken directly by God. Whether a matter in the past or present, it is always continuously active.

Appendix "A": Psalm 119 Study Aids

Psalm 119

There are 8 different words used throughout Psalm 119 to describe God's Word. Make sure of their definition each time they are used, & the correct context in which they are employed. These are **NOT** synonyms with the same meaning, but each communicate something very specific.

Command-ment ("Mitsvah")	Law ("Torah")	Ordinance/ Judgment ("Mishpat")	Precept ("Piqqud")	Statute ("Choq"/ "Chuqqah")	Testimony ("Edah"/ "Eduth")	Ways ("Derek"/ "Orach")	Word ("Dabar"/ "Imrah")
Used 22 Times	Used 25 Times	Used 20 Times	Used 21 Times	Used 22 Times	Used 25 Times	Used 7 Times	Used 25 Times
Requirements for living in a covenant relationship with God.	"Torah" is not only the name of the Law, but also means "teaching" or "instruction".	What we might call "case law", the application of God's Word in situations not specifically addressed in Scripture word-for-word.	From Hebrew word for "inspect". The requirements of God's people AFTER entering into a covenant relationship with Him.	Prescribed tasks and boundaries of a permanent nature, such as rules for holy days, sacrifices, limits on marriage, etc.	"Eye witness" testimony. God's personal corroboration of the benefits and/or consequences where His Word is concerned.	Refers to a well-traveled road. The course which God reveals as right & which humans stick to or stray from.	A matter or cause spoken directly by God. Whether a matter in the past or present, it is always continuously active.

Psalm 119

There are 8 different words used throughout Psalm 119 to describe God's Word. Make sure of their definition each time they are used, & the correct context in which they are employed. These are **NOT** synonyms with the same meaning, but each communicate something very specific.

Command-ment ("Mitsvah")	Law ("Torah")	Ordinance/ Judgment ("Mishpat")	Precept ("Piqqud")	Statute ("Choq"/ "Chuqqah")	Testimony ("Edah"/ "Eduth")	Ways ("Derek"/ "Orach")	Word ("Dabar"/ "Imrah")
Used 22 Times	Used 25 Times	Used 20 Times	Used 21 Times	Used 22 Times	Used 25 Times	Used 7 Times	Used 25 Times
Requirements for living in a covenant relationship with God.	"Torah" is not only the name of the Law, but also means "teaching" or "instruction".	What we might call "case law", the application of God's Word in situations not specifically addressed in Scripture word-for-word.	From Hebrew word for "inspect". The requirements of God's people AFTER entering into a covenant relationship with Him.	Prescribed tasks and boundaries of a permanent nature, such as rules for holy days, sacrifices, limits on marriage, etc.	"Eye witness" testimony. God's personal corroboration of the benefits and/or consequences where His Word is concerned.	Refers to a well-traveled road. The course which God reveals as right & which humans stick to or stray from.	A matter or cause spoken directly by God. Whether a matter in the past or present, it is always continuously active.

Psalm 119

There are 8 different words used throughout Psalm 119 to describe God's Word. Make sure of their definition each time they are used, & the correct context in which they are employed. These are **NOT** synonyms with the same meaning, but each communicate something very specific.

Command-ment ("Mitsvah")	Law ("Torah")	Ordinance/ Judgment ("Mishpat")	Precept ("Piqqud")	Statute ("Choq"/ "Chuqqah")	Testimony ("Edah"/ "Eduth")	Ways ("Derek"/ "Orach")	Word ("Dabar"/ "Imrah")
Used 22 Times	Used 25 Times	Used 20 Times	Used 21 Times	Used 22 Times	Used 25 Times	Used 7 Times	Used 25 Times
Requirements for living in a covenant relationship with God.	"Torah" is not only the name of the Law, but also means "teaching" or "instruction".	What we might call "case law", the application of God's Word in situations not specifically addressed in Scripture word-for-word.	From Hebrew word for "inspect". The requirements of God's people AFTER entering into a covenant relationship with Him.	Prescribed tasks and boundaries of a permanent nature, such as rules for holy days, sacrifices, limits on marriage, etc.	"Eye witness" testimony. God's personal corroboration of the benefits and/or consequences where His Word is concerned.	Refers to a well-traveled road. The course which God reveals as right & which humans stick to or stray from.	A matter or cause spoken directly by God. Whether a matter in the past or present, it is always continuously active.

Psalm 119

There are 8 different words used throughout Psalm 119 to describe God's Word. Make sure of their definition each time they are used, & the correct context in which they are employed. These are **NOT** synonyms with the same meaning, but each communicate something very specific.

Command-ment ("Mitsvah")	Law ("Torah")	Ordinance/ Judgment ("Mishpat")	Precept ("Piqqud")	Statute ("Choq"/ "Chuqqah")	Testimony ("Edah"/ "Eduth")	Ways ("Derek"/ "Orach")	Word ("Dabar"/ "Imrah")
Used 22 Times	Used 25 Times	Used 20 Times	Used 21 Times	Used 22 Times	Used 25 Times	Used 7 Times	Used 25 Times
Requirements for living in a covenant relationship with God.	"Torah" is not only the name of the Law, but also means "teaching" or "instruction".	What we might call "case law", the application of God's Word in situations not specifically addressed in Scripture word-for-word.	From Hebrew word for "inspect". The requirements of God's people AFTER entering into a covenant relationship with Him.	Prescribed tasks and boundaries of a permanent nature, such as rules for holy days, sacrifices, limits on marriage, etc.	"Eye witness" testimony. God's personal corroboration of the benefits and/or consequences where His Word is concerned.	Refers to a well-traveled road. The course which God reveals as right & which humans stick to or stray from.	A matter or cause spoken directly by God. Whether a matter in the past or present, it is always continuously active.

Appendix "B": The Inductive Bible Study Method

The Inductive Bible Study method is applicable to every level from individual study, to leading a small group, to teaching children's Sunday School, to the main message coming from the pulpit. It's goal is to provide a framework by which you can hear God speaking through His Word and make personal application to your life. It's how one becomes a ***doer*** of the Word and not just a ***listener***. This brief introduction is essential to understanding Walk with the Word's perspective and approach to providing Bible studies and related materials to all levels of ministry. There are many books and web sites devoted to this topic which will provide much more detail if desired. (One such resource we highly recommend is provided by Intensive Care Ministries at www.icmbible.com.) The following is provided as an overview.

At its simplest, the Inductive method employs three basic techniques:

- Observation
- Interpretation
- Application

Observation

Observation teaches you to see what the passage says and is the basis for accurate interpretation and correct application. It is vitally important to understand the context of the Scripture being studied and to not pull the words or sentences away from their true meaning. Observation answers the question, "What does the passage say?"

You don't have to earn a degree in Greek, Hebrew and Aramaic to figure out the correct context of any portion of Scripture. (Can't hurt, either.) But it's essential that you keep in mind that language changes over time, and that speech patterns, writing styles, and communication methods differ during the course of our own lifetime, much less over 2,000 years and many, many cultural hand-offs. The observation techniques which follow allow you to glean what is being said in the proper context as you study.

Begin with prayer.

If you want to "hear" what God has to say to you personally, you really need to enter into two-way communication. Prayer ***begins*** the "conversation" and places your mind, heart and soul in the right relationship with Him.

Ask the 5 W's and an H.

The hardest thing to do is ridding ourselves of assumptions when we approach God's Word, whether it's a book ("Revelation is nothing but symbols and allegories.") or a familiar passage ("1 Corinthians 13 is all I need to know about 'love.'"). Presuppositions are the most common culprits leading to wrong interpretation and misapplication. Carefully observing who, what, when, where, why and how are the best assurances leading to correct interpretation. **DON'T RUSH PAST THIS**. Doing this on a chapter-by-chapter basis consistently places the paragraphs, sentences, and words in their proper context.

- **WHO** is speaking? Who is this about? Who are the main characters? ***To Whom*** is he speaking? A person may not be named but identified by their character. (e.g., "arrogant", "faithful", etc.) Pay attention to the pronouns. (e.g., "he", "she", "it", "them", etc.) Does the person's name have a special meaning?

- **WHAT** is the subject or event covered in the chapter? What do you learn about the people, event, or teaching? What is taking place? What is being said and to what is it referring?

- **WHEN** do/will the events occur or did/will something happen to someone in particular?

- **WHERE** did or will this happen? Where was it said? Does the name of the location hold a special meaning or have a relevant history?

- **WHY** is something being said or mentioned? Why would/will this happen? Why at that time and/or to this person/people/place/thing?

- **HOW** will it happen? How is it to be done? How is it illustrated?

Mark key words and phrases.

A keyword or phrase is one which, when removed, leaves the passage void of meaning. They are often repeated by the author throughout a chapter or book in order to reveal the point or purpose of the writing.

However you decide to mark such things in your Bible, determine to be consistent in your use of colors, symbols, or a combination of both throughout in order to capture important themes which transcend just a single passage of Scripture. (e.g. "love", "covenant", "sin", "grace", etc.)

Pay attention to pronouns ("he", "she", "we", "they", "I", "you", "it", "our", etc.) as they often indicate a change of direction or emphasis. (e.g., when it changes from "He" says to "you" say.) And note synonyms which are different ways to referring to the same person, place, or thing. For instance, there are many names for "God", several names for "Jerusalem", and so on. These often hint at different character traits of the same entity, trying to teach us a little more about it. Alternate descriptions of the same thing are most often highlighting a different, important spiritual aspect or character trait important to the context.

Look for lists.

Trivia Time: In movies, books and everyday speech people often refer to "The Seven Deadly Sins" – where did that come from? One of Paul's epistles. (Looking it up would be good for you.) Lists are often additional words used to describe a keyword or subject, but are also what is said about someone or something, or related thoughts/instructions grouped together.

Lists are something you should develop as you study a particular topic throughout the Bible such as "faith". Listing the characteristics of faith as provided by each use throughout Scripture will provide you with a much broader view of the whole meaning of faith. Such a list allows you see the bigger picture and avoid incorrectly interpreting it on the basis of just one Scripture in and of itself. Lists are the building blocks to developing something usually described in the much more intimidating terms "doctrine" and "theology".

Yes, keeping lists of the important topics provides you with the basis for personalizing doctrines and theologies which follow from studying a theme across the entire Bible. Essentially you are placing the foundation layers of your faith into their right and proper context.

Watch for contrasts and comparisons.

A *contrast* is a comparison of things that are different or opposite, such as light/darkness, proud/humble, good/evil. The word "but" often indicates a contrast to something just stated.

A *comparison* points out similarities and is most often indicated in the use of words such as like, as, as it were.

These small words are great eye-openers in the process of observation as they set the words on either side of them into their proper context.

Identify terms of conclusion.

Wherefore, therefore, for this reason, and *finally* are terms of conclusion which usually follow an important thought in order to tell you how to personally apply the teaching. They're a bridge between the "teaching" and the "application" and often clearly spell out the proper meaning and context of the passage with no guesswork as to what it means.

Develop your own chapter themes.

The printed chapter themes in most Bibles are more of an aid for finding a specific story or passage such as "Jesus Heals a Blind Man"; they're not very descriptive of the spiritual topic or theme which reveal the lessons God is directing to your heart. Nearly every Bible translation is available without such markings, usually in a "wide margin" edition conducive to making personal notes. *The New Inductive Study Bible* by Harvest House Publishers, for instance, builds this into several versions and even provides a place at the end of every book to record your personal chapter headings in order to see patterns and development of themes. But this can also easily be maintained on a separate sheet of paper.

But also recognize that in the original texts, they were never annotated with verse and chapter markings. Although this addition is greatly beneficial overall, they don't always divide chapters, and sometimes even verses, in the right place. Sometimes a theme actually extends just past or begins just before the chapter marking in your Bible, so don't hesitate to make such adjustments as needed.

Note expressions of time.

This is often the most-overlooked part of observation. A crucial part of attaining the correct context is understanding when something has/is/will happen.

Time is often directly indicated such as "during the reign of", "on the tenth day", "at the feast of", etc., etc. Sometimes the context is as much about when, or its relationship to a past or present event, as it is the person, place or thing mentioned.

Pay attention to words such as *until, then, when,* and *after* as they reveal the relationship of one event to another. This is of particular importance when studying the Gospels as you will begin to see that Jesus' actions and miracles are often an extension of the teaching He gave just before or after them. Throughout the Bible these words help connect actions with teaching in the proper context.

When dealing with the prophetic portions of God's Word, it is essential to understand that while there is almost always a literal, historical meaning for the time at which it was originally given, there is also possible additional meanings which apply to Christ's First Coming, His Second Coming, or both. This is often revealed by paying close attention to observing all the accompanying time indicators related to "when".

These are the fundamentals and, to be sure, there are added guidelines for the proper observation applied to some of the different types of literature provided throughout the Bible such as psalms, songs, parables, allegories, etc. But this will serve as the baseline throughout.

Proper observation takes the guesswork out of interpretation and application. As stated previously, don't rush through observation because you want to get to interpretation or application more quickly. The latter are only properly achieved through patient and thorough observation.

Appendix "B": The Inductive Bible Study Method

2. Interpretation

Interpretation answers the question, "What does the passage mean?" Tons of books and web sites are available on this topic—not to mention hundreds of institutions providing degrees in related fields—so these are the basic rules. But don't let anyone intimidate you from following these steps; God makes known His knowledge and will to **ANYONE** who seeks. (This is a good topic for you to keep track of throughout your studies.)

- ***Context ALWAYS rules first.*** Never take a Scripture out of its context to make it say what *you* want it to say. Look at context first from the perspective of the book being studied, the overall chapter, the paragraph, and the sentence. Try to stay away from giving individual words meanings that reinterpret sentences, paragraphs, and onward up.

- ***Always seek the FULL counsel of God's Word.*** Never accept someone's teaching based on one or two verses; ensure that they're not taken out of context as they're employed throughout the whole Bible.

- ***Scripture never contradicts Scripture.*** It's amazing how the best interpreter of Scripture is other Scripture. One of the best study aids is a good concordance and Bible dictionary which will show words and concepts as they're presented throughout **ALL** of Scripture. This is often the best use of footnotes in your Bible indicating other verses utilizing the same words or phrases in other places so you can compare and contrast how it's used in many passages.

- ***Never base a belief or conviction on an obscure passage of Scripture.*** You can always ask other Believers, go to Bible dictionaries or commentaries, or submit it to God in prayer and await His direction.

- ***Interpret Scripture literally.*** Obviously there are no dragons and the Bible uses it and other symbols. But these are far and away the exceptions in the Bible as the vast majority are very, very literal. Beware of false teachers who teach that *the whole* Bible is just allegory, such as Jonah and the big fish, or the Garden of Eden, etc., etc. This is an error called "spiritualizing" the text. These and all events, places and things in the Bible are real and not allegory. God is very clear in Scripture when He uses allegory, parables, or other literary devices to communicate His Word.

- ***Begin with the primary meaning of the passage.*** Let the passage speak for itself. Seek to understand what the author had in mind. Flee from those that teach about things such as "Bible codes" or try to twist Scripture to support a meaning it never had in the first place. Making something complicated is usually an outward sign of someone who is going to great lengths to justify some kind of sin in their life, or the choices they've made, or a false teaching. Keep in mind that allegories and typology always *illuminate* what is already present in Scripture—they are never used as the *basis* for doctrine but to support and explain it in harmony with the rest of God's Word.

- ***The NT has priority.*** A long-time rule of interpretation is expressed in the saying, "The 'New' is in the 'Old' concealed, the 'Old' is in the 'New' revealed". In other words, what was initially set forth in the Old Testament is brought to light and fulfillment in the New Testament.

3. Application

Application answers the question, "How should I apply this personally? What truths can I put into practice? What changes should I make to my life?"

Paul states in 2 Timothy 3:16-17, *"All Scripture is inspired by God and profitable for teaching, for reproof, for correction, for training in righteousness, so that the man of God may be adequate, equipped for every good work."* Paul provides the activities involved in application: Teaching, reproof, correction, and training in righteousness. Notice how they are focused on our behavior.

- **Teaching** is what the Word of God has to say on any topic or subject and is always true. Once you discover what the Word of God teaches, you are obligated before God to accept that truth and to live by it, dropping any false beliefs or teachings you may have previously held.

- **Reproof** is finding out where you have thought or behaved wrongly or have not been doing what God says is right according to His Word. It's your personal acknowledgment that you were wrong in thought or behavior and now accept and agree with God's truth, setting you free from sin and unbelief.

- **Correction** is the step wherein the knowledge gained from teaching and reproof are placed into action resulting in changed behavior. It's converting knowledge into obedience.

- **Training in righteousness** can be thought of in terms of God's Word as a handbook for living, for how we conduct ourselves. It's continually returning to the source and consistently putting into practice the reproofs and corrections of His Word to build our character in Him.

In seeking to apply Scripture to your life, ask the following questions in light of your observation and interpretation:

- What does the passage teach?

- As I've studied this passage, do any errors in my belief or problems with my behavior come to mind?

- Remembering that God is my Father and I am His child, what instruction is my Father trying to pass to me, His child?

Finally, in the process of applying Scripture, take note to beware of the following:

- Applying cultural standards rather than biblical standards.

- Attempting to strengthen a legitimate truth by using Scripture incorrectly.

- Applying Scripture out of prejudice from past training or teaching.

Conclusion

Observation, interpretation, and application lead to *transformation*. This is the goal at every level of Bible teaching whether in an individual's daily devotions or the Sunday morning sermon. This is the process of becoming more and more like the image of Christ that we might not only enjoy a deeper personal relationship with

Appendix "B": The Inductive Bible Study Method

our Savior but reflect His image to the world rather than our own. Or as Christ described it, becoming doers of the Law.

But there is probably no better scriptural explanation for why we pursue the application of God's Word to our life, behavior, and even thoughts than the ultimate goal of not just experiencing, but in turn *being*, a vessel of Christ's love:

> "This is My commandment, that you love one another, just as I have loved you. — John 15:12

Jesus specifically provides an explanation as to the means by which this highest standard of love comes about in a believer's life:

> Jesus answered and said to him, "**If anyone loves Me, he will keep My word**; and My Father will love him, and We will come to him and make Our abode with him. **He who does not love Me does not keep My words**; and the word which you hear is not Mine, but the Father's who sent Me. — John 14:23–24

The specific process of how you can accomplish this through God's Word is provided in more detail by the Apostle Paul:

> But the goal of our instruction is love from a pure heart and a good conscience and a sincere faith. — 1 Timothy 1:5

"*Love*" is the very goal of God's Word, but it only comes about with the proper application in very specific ways.

- **"A pure heart"**. The biblical definition of "*pure*" can best be thought of as "unpolluted by sin". This is describing an absolute intolerance for the allowance of personal sin. God's Word provides the descriptions and parameters of sin. To "*love from a pure heart*" requires the application of God's Word to your heart.

- **"A good conscience"**. This moves to the mind where all things are evaluated as to whether they are God's way, our way, or the world's way. Cartoons often depict this as an angel on one shoulder and a demon on the other, with a choice to be made as to which one will be followed. God's Word provides the truth so that we can distinguish the difference. But "*a **good** conscience*" is one which always choose God's way regardless. This requires the application of God's Word to your mind.

- **"A sincere faith"**. In both Testaments, the word "*faith*" can be rendered in English either as "faith" or "faithfulness". Another way of stating this is to be "sincerely faithful"—that is, never straying from God's path. The Holy Spirit through God's Word constantly guides us in this regard. To consistently maintain "*a sincere faith*" requires the application of God's Word to your soul.

The reason we find it so difficult to love like Christ is because we are usually found to be compromised in one or more of these areas. Even though we may properly deal with **some** sin, we still make allowances; though we **usually** choose to do the right and biblical thing, we often choose the alternative; though we **mostly** stick to the right path, at times we take detours, however small. We fall short in the ability to love like Christ because we fail to fully apply and abide by God's Word from the heart, mind and soul. Biblical love is not listed as a spiritual gift or ever given to someone supernaturally because it stems from how one handles and uncompromisingly puts into practice the entire Word of God at every level of our being.

Reading the Bible is not some kind of added bonus which God has given us, but it is the way by which His salvation, justification and sanctification are accomplished. This goes hand-in-hand with Christ's teaching of the true, ultimate goal of not just knowing His Word, but putting it into practice:

"If you love Me, you will keep My commandments. — John 14:15

"He who has My commandments and keeps them is the one who loves Me; and he who loves Me will be loved by My Father, and I will love him and will disclose Myself to him." — John 14:21

"If you keep My commandments, you will abide in My love; just as I have kept My Father's commandments and abide in His love. — John 15:10

Studying the Bible inductively is not dedicated to mining information, but fulfilling biblical love both in and through us by not simply reading the text, but putting His Word into practice so to tangibly change us accordingly.

[Note: The following page can be printed out and folded in thirds to keep as a study sheet in your Bible. Prints on normal 8-1/2 x 11 paper, but requires trimming the margin. If desired, a color version is available as a free download from the Walk with the Word website. (www.WalkWithTheWord.org)]

Appendix "B": The Inductive Bible Study Method

Interpretation

Answers the question, "What does the passage mean?"

Follow these basic rules:

1. Remember that context always rules first.
2. Always seek the full counsel of the Word of God. (Compare and contrast similar passages.)
3. Remember that Scripture will never contradict Scripture.
4. Don't base your convictions on an obscure passage of Scripture.
5. Interpret Scripture literally.
6. Allegories and typology are used to illustrate & confirm, never the basis to replace and/or create.
7. The NT has priority.

Application

Answers the question, "What does it mean to me personally? What truths can I put into practice? What changes should I make to my life?"

> *"All Scripture is inspired by God and profitable for teaching, for reproof, for correction, for training in righteousness, so that the man of God may be adequate, equipped for every good work."*
> 2 Timonthy 3:16-17 (NASB)

Inductive Study Approach

To facilitate "hearing" God's Word as you study, the Inductive Study Approach employs three basic, sequential techniques:
- Observation
- Interpretation
- Application

Observation

Teaches you to see what the passage says and is the basis for accurate interpretation & correct application. Observation answers the question, "What does the passage say?"

Step 1: Begin with Prayer

Step 2: Ask the "5 W's & an H"
- ☐ **Who** is speaking? Who is this about? Who are the main characters? To whom are they speaking?
- ☐ **What** is the subject or event covered in the chapter? What do you learn about the people, event or teaching?
- ☐ **When** do/will the events occur or do/will something happen to someone in particular?
- ☐ **Where** did or will this happen? Where was it said? Does the location have a relevant past or future mention elsewhere in Scripture?
- ☐ **Why** is something being said or mentioned? Why would/will this happen? Why at that time/to this person/in that place?
- ☐ **How** will it happen? How is it illustrated?

Step 3: Mark Keywords & Phrases

Step 4: Look for Lists

Step 5: Watch for Contrasts & Comparisons

Step 6: Note Expressions of Time
(Don't forget "until", "then", "when", etc.)

Step 7: Identify Terms of Conclusion
("wherefore", "finally", "for this reason", "therefore", "so", etc.)

Step 8: Develop Chapter Themes
Ignore the ones printed in your Bible and instead write in the margin the theme YOU see, centering on the main person, event, teaching or subject of Scripture. (Sometimes themes span chapters.)

Psalm 119

There are 8 different words used throughout Psalm 119 to describe God's Word. Make sure of their definition each time they are used, & the correct context in which they are employed. These are **NOT** synonyms with the same meaning, but each communicate something very specific.

Command-ment ("Mitsvah")	Law ("Torah")	Ordinance/ Judgment ("Mishpat")	Precept ("Piqqud")	Statute ("Choq"/ "Chuqqah")	Testimony ("Edah"/ "Eduth")	Ways ("Derek"/ "Orach")	Word ("Dabar"/ "Imrah")
Used 22 Times	Used 25 Times	Used 20 Times	Used 21 Times	Used 22 Times	Used 25 Times	Used 7 Times	Used 25 Times
Requirements for living in a covenant relationship with God.	"Torah" is not only the name of the Law, but also means "teaching" or "instruction".	What we might call "case law", the application of God's Word in situations not specifically addressed in Scripture word-for-word.	From Hebrew word for "inspect". The requirements of God's people AFTER entering into a covenant relationship with Him.	Prescribed tasks and boundaries of a permanent nature, such as rules for holy days, sacrifices, limits on marriage, etc.	"Eye witness" testimony. God's personal corroboration of the benefits and/or consequences where His Word is concerned.	Refers to a well-traveled road. The course which God reveals as right & which humans stick to or stray from.	A matter or cause spoken directly by God. Whether a matter in the past or present, it is always continuously active.

Appendix "C": Small Group Materials

Small Group Leader Study Notes

What follows are notes for leading a small group or seminar through Psalm 119 two or three stanzas per lesson. These are designed more for guiding an open discussion than preaching a straightforward sermon. In a small group environment, the whole of Psalm 119 is covered in eight lessons. The leader's goal is to guide the discussion so that each participant arrives at the point wherein they realize how the Holy Spirit is speaking to them personally through the text. The discussion should never devolve to, "This is what it means to me", but remain centered on, "This is what I'm being convicted to do with it".

Following these notes are the "Small Group Handouts" in a fill-in-the-blanks format. There is an answer key for the leader and a corresponding handout for participants. All of these materials are supplied with the intention that the leader will make copies as needed for the group participants, but are not necessary if they are using the companion printed workbook.

Psalm 119:1-8, 9-16, & 17-24 • Aleph, Beth & Gimel (#1-3)

Introduction

[Note: Each stanza of Psalm 119 is a study in and of itself. For the purposes of leading a small group study, these three are presented together as a single study.]

It should not surprise anyone that Psalm 119 is the largest of the 929 chapters in our Bible as it is dedicated to not only explaining how Scripture is organized by its consistent use of 8 categories of God's Word, but repeatedly provides real world examples of how we are to apply every facet of God's Word to our life. The goal is not to determine what we can expect from God's Word, but that which we need to do to meet the personal shortfalls of what God's Word expects from us.

¹How blessed are those whose way is blameless,
Who walk in the law of the LORD.
²How blessed are those who observe His testimonies,
Who seek Him with all their heart.
³They also do no unrighteousness;
They walk in His ways.
⁴You have ordained Your precepts,
That we should keep them diligently.
⁵Oh that my ways may be established
To keep Your statutes!
⁶Then I shall not be ashamed
When I look upon all Your commandments.
⁷I shall give thanks to You with uprightness of heart,
When I learn Your righteous judgments.
⁸I shall keep Your statutes;
Do not forsake me utterly!

[Read v.1-8] My Way is His Way

Q: Who is "blessed"?
   A: "*...those...who walk in the law*" (v.1) and "*observe His testimonies*" (v.2)—not just His instructions, but His affirming testimony of the benefits and requirements of His Word.

Q: Is this an unconditional state of blessedness?
   A: It is experienced by those who are "*blameless*" only because of walking in, observing and seeking from the heart the pursuit of obedience to God's Word.

Q: How is the behavior of such a person visibly proven?
   A: They "*...do no unrighteousness*" (v.3). Truly keeping God's Word is always reflected in the quality of one's behavior.

Q: Why are "statutes" connected with "commandments" in v.5-6?
   A: The OT Covenant included commandments whose requirements could not be met without properly observing the rituals, observances and sacrifices detailed in God's Word. "*Commandments*" provide the requirement, "*statues*" specify how to carry it out.

Q: What is the personal effect when a believer does not keep His Word?
   A: They experience shame (v.6) as His Word identifies their personal shortcomings in this regard.

Q: What is v.7 referring to?
A: The application of God's Word so as to be obedient in all things, properly applying God's Word even when a situation is not specifically spelled out word-for-word in Scripture.

Q: What is the potential result of a lack of obedience to His Word?
A: Being utterly forsaken. (v.8)

Application: *The way by which to walk "blameless" in Christ is to put into practice His ways as specified by His Word. This will not only be evident in our personal relationship with Him, but reflected in our visible behavior and witness to others.*

[Read v.9-16] Staying & Not Straying

Q: What is the main issue raised in v.9?
A: Keeping *"pure"*. This is the scriptural way of characterizing someone as being "unpolluted by sin". This can only be accomplished by not straying from God's Word. (Especially an issue for a *"young man"*.)

> [9] How can a young man keep his way pure?
> By keeping it according to Your word.
> [10] With all my heart I have sought You;
> Do not let me wander from Your commandments.
> [11] Your word I have treasured in my heart,
> That I may not sin against You.
> [12] Blessed are You, O LORD;
> Teach me Your statutes.
> [13] With my lips I have told of
> All the ordinances of Your mouth.
> [14] I have rejoiced in the way of Your testimonies,
> As much as in all riches.
> [15] I will meditate on Your precepts
> And regard Your ways.
> [16] I shall delight in Your statutes;
> I shall not forget Your word.

Q: How is this evidenced in the following verses?
A: The ability to *"not sin against You"* is only possible in someone who does not *"wander from Your commandments"* (v.10) and treasures God's Word *"in my heart"*. It describes someone who behaves and practices what is truly within them. (Jesus said in Mt. 15:17-20 it is what comes out of someone which proves his inner spiritual state.)

Q: What is the list of actions properly taken in v.9-13?

- *"Keeping"* (v.9)
- *"Sought"* (v.10)
- *"Treasured"* (v.11)
- Testimony (*"I have told"*) (v.13)

We must be active both personally in our internal pursuit of a relationship with Christ, as well as externally as a visible example and testimony of the working of His Word to others through us.

Q: What is the contrast between v.10 & 14?
  A: A true seeker from the heart does not confuse it with the earthly pursuit of material gain, which is one of the primary tools of sin.

Q: What is most likely listed as the greatest danger?
  A: *"Do not let me wander"* (V.10) so as to avoid sin.

Q: How is this followed up with a list of appropriate responses in v. 14-16?

- *"...rejoiced in...Your testimonies"* (v.14)—that is, the right response to God's affirmation of both the consequence and benefits associated with His Word.

- *"...meditate on Your precepts"* (v.15)—that is, obedience to those things for which believers are responsible after coming into a covenant relationship with God.

- *"...regard Your ways"* (v.15)—that is, seriously remaining on the path of God's Word.

- *"...delight in Your statutes"* (v.16)—that is, view positively the benefits of the boundaries and restrictions specified in God's Word.

- *"...not forget Your word"* (v.16)—that is, to bring to every decision, situation and relationship the application of God's Word for each and every thing.

Application: *Obedience to God's Word is the remedy for both wandering from God's path and preventing the allowance of the inevitable pollution of sin.*

> ¹⁷Deal bountifully with Your servant,
> That I may live and keep Your word.
> ¹⁸Open my eyes, that I may behold
> Wonderful things from Your law.
> ¹⁹I am a stranger in the earth;
> Do not hide Your commandments from me.
> ²⁰My soul is crushed with longing
> After Your ordinances at all times.
> ²¹You rebuke the arrogant, the cursed,
> Who wander from Your commandments.
> ²²Take away reproach and contempt from me,
> For I observe Your testimonies.
> ²³Even though princes sit and talk against me,
> Your servant meditates on Your statutes.
> ²⁴Your testimonies also are my delight;
> They are my counselors.

[Read v.17-24] The Earthly vs. the Heavenly

Q: Who are the people mentioned here? (Not every person has a proper name or stated position.)

- *"Your servant"* (v.17)
- *"a stranger in the earth"* (v.19)
- *"the arrogant"* (v.21)
- *"the cursed"* (v.21)
- *"princes"* (v.23)
- *"counselors"* (v.24)

Q: How are these figures being compared and contrasted to each other?

A: One who puts God's Word into practice is not only a *"servant"*—in the service of and indebted to the Master, but is *"a stranger on earth"*—that is, no longer a citizen of the earthly but rather the heavenly. They are no longer following the wisdom and advice of those still belonging to the earthly, who are here characterized as *"the arrogant"*, those who are ignorant of God's Word and ways, or even having a position of earthly authority such as *"princes"*.

Q: What do the earthly heap upon those focused on God's Word?

A: *"...reproach and contempt..."* (v.22) This is to be the expected response from the earthly to those in obedience to God's Word.

Q: How does this situation highlight the believer's personal character trait, "My soul is crushed with longing after Your ordinances at all times"? (v.20)

A: An ordinance is the application of God's Word in all things, particularly those which are not categorically spelled out word-for-word in the text of Scripture. It is erring on the side of God's Word where all things are concerned.

Application: *We should not be living as an earthly resident following its ways and listening to its messengers, but as "a stranger in the earth" who in all things regards God's Word as "my counselors".*

Overall Application

Q: What do these three teachings have in common?

A: We not only no longer live according to our own life, but neither do we live by the world's standards.

Q: How do we know what standards to pursue?
A: God's Word.

Application: *How well do you realize that your personal struggles in your Christian walk may be related to how you approach and handle God's Word? How might the Word be able to deal with such issues? Discuss how this works for...*

- We go to the Word to maintain a *"blameless"* walk both with Christ and others.

- We go to the Word to prevent our wandering and allowance of sin.

- We go to the Word as our personal guidance counselor.

Psalm 119 • Master for Handout (#1-3)

1. **Aleph (א): My Way is His Way** (v.1-8) The way by which to walk "**blameless**" in Christ is to put into practice His ways as specified by His **Word**. This will not only be evident in our personal relationship with **Him**, but reflected in our visible behavior and witness to **others**.

2. **Beth (ב): Staying & Not Straying** (v.9-16) **Obedience** to God's Word is the remedy for both wandering from God's **path** and preventing the allowance of the inevitable pollution of **sin**.

3. **Gimel (ג): The Earthly vs. the Heavenly** (v.17-24) We should not be living as an **earthly** resident following its ways and listening to its **messengers**, but as "a **stranger** in the earth" who in all things regards God's Word as "my **counselors**".

For Small Group Leaders to summarize these three lessons:

Overall Application

Q: What do these three teachings have in common?
A: We not only no longer according to our life, but neither do we live by the world's standards.

Q: How do we know what standards to pursue?
A: God's Word.

Application: How well do you realize that your personal struggles in your Christian walk may be related to how you handle God's Word? How might the Word be able to deal with such issues? Discuss how this works for...

- We go to the Word to maintain a "**blameless**" walk both with Christ and others.

- We go to the Word to prevent our **wandering** and allowance of **sin**.

- We go to the Word as our personal guidance **counselor**.

Psalm 119 Group Handout • Aleph, Beth & Gimel (#1-3)

1. **Aleph (א): My Way is His Way** (v.1-8) The way by which to walk "_____" in Christ is to put into practice His ways as specified by His _____. This will not only be evident in our personal relationship with _____, but reflected in our visible behavior and witness to _____.

2. **Beth (ב): Staying & Not Straying** (v.9-16) _____ to God's Word is the remedy for both wandering from God's _____ and preventing the allowance of the inevitable pollution of _____.

3. **Gimel (ג): The Earthly vs. the Heavenly** (v.17-24) We should not be living as an _____ resident following its ways and listening to its _____, but as "a _____ in the earth" who in all things regards God's Word as "my _____."

Overall Application

- We go to the Word to maintain a "_____" walk both with Christ and others.
- We go to the Word to prevent our _____ and allowance of _____.
- We go to the Word as our personal guidance _____.

Psalm 119:25-32, 33-40, 41-48 • Daleth, He & Vav (#4-6)

Introduction

[Note: Each stanza of Psalm 119 is a study in and of itself. For the purposes of leading a small group study, these three are presented together as a single study.]

It should not surprise anyone that Psalm 119 is the largest of the 929 chapters in our Bible as it is dedicated to not only explaining how Scripture is organized by its consistent use of 8 categories of God's Word, but repeatedly provides real world examples of how we are to apply every facet of God's Word to our life. The goal is not to determine what we can expect from God's Word, but that which we need to do to meet the personal shortfalls of what God's Word expects from us.

> ²⁵My soul cleaves to the dust;
> Revive me according to Your word.
> ²⁶I have told of my ways, and You have answered me;
> Teach me Your statutes.
> ²⁷Make me understand the way of Your precepts,
> So I will meditate on Your wonders.
> ²⁸My soul weeps because of grief;
> Strengthen me according to Your word.
> ²⁹Remove the false way from me,
> And graciously grant me Your law.
> ³⁰I have chosen the faithful way;
> I have placed Your ordinances before me.
> ³¹I cling to Your testimonies; O LORD, do not put me to shame!
> ³²I shall run the way of Your commandments,
> For You will enlarge my heart.

[Read v.25-32] A Cure for the Blues

Q: How does the Psalm's author describe his personal condition?

- *"My soul cleaves to the dust…"* (v.25)
- *"My soul weeps because of grief…"* (v.28)

He is at a very low point both emotionally and spiritually.

Q: What is the good news regarding this according to v.26?

A: *"I have told of my ways, and You have answered me"*. He has received a response from the Lord.

Q: What is the nature of that response? Was it to perform a miracle or invoke divine intervention?

A: Encouragement to obey God's Word regardless.

Q: What are the keywords in v.25-29 which provide a basic structure of a prayer which God will always answer?

- *"Revive me"* (v.25)
- *"Teach me"* (v.26)
- *"Make me understand"* (v.27)
- *"Strengthen me"* (v.28)
- *"Remove the false way from me"* (v.29)

Notice that these are all fulfilled by obedience and commitment to His Word, not by any kind of supernatural response.

Q: What is the primary benefit which is specified here for obedience to God's Word in spite of one's personal emotional state?

A: *"For You will enlarge my heart"*. (v.32)

Application: *Obedience to God's Word and ways even when one is personally and emotionally low provides the appropriate remedy where it matters most: the heart.*

[Read v.33-40] The Biblical Definition of Revival

Q: What are the related phrases in this passage which have in common the writer's desire for God's direction where His Word is concerned?

- (v.33) *"Teach me"*
- (v.34) *"Give me understanding"*
- (v.35) *"Make me walk in the path"*
- (v.36) *"Incline my heart"*
- (v.38) *"Establish Your word to Your servant"*

Q: What are the desired results which reveal that this is not so much about knowledge as it is about faithfulness?

- (v.33) *"...I shall observe it to the end."*
- (v.34) *"...that I may observe Your law..."*
- (v.34) *"...that I may...keep it with all my heart."*
- (v.35) *"...produces reverence for You."*

Q: What are the potential pitfalls or obstacles that the writer desires to simultaneously overcome or avoid?

- (v.36) *"Incline my heart...not to dishonest gain."*
- (v.37) *"Turn away my eyes from looking at vanity..."*
- (v.39) *"Turn away reproach..."*

Point: *Note how these items are issues of pride and the flesh which bring our attention down to this present life and living for ourselves, the diametric opposite of what takes place when we allow God's Word to take hold.*

---

³³Teach me, O LORD, the way of Your statutes,
And I shall observe it to the end.
³⁴Give me understanding, that I may observe Your law
And keep it with all my heart.
³⁵Make me walk in the path of Your commandments,
For I delight in it.
³⁶Incline my heart to Your testimonies
And not to dishonest gain.
³⁷Turn away my eyes from looking at vanity,
And revive me in Your ways.
³⁸Establish Your word to Your servant,
As that which produces reverence for You.
³⁹Turn away my reproach which I dread,
For Your ordinances are good.
⁴⁰Behold, I long for Your precepts;
Revive me through Your righteousness.

Q: What is probably the repeated keyword in these verses? What important definition is it providing within the overall context?

A: *"Revive"*. (v.37, 40) The definition of a true "revival" is not the unsaved coming to the Lord, but the backslidden.

Application: Note how these combine to describe a lifestyle of putting God's Word into practice and not merely obtaining knowledge.

[Read v.41-48] The Cycle of the Word in the Saved

Q: What is the dual nature of the working of God's Word where the believer is concerned in v.41-43?

A: In one's personal relationship with Christ it is grace and salvation, but where earthly relationships are concerned they are equally critical.

Q: How would this relate to the statement, "For I will wait for Your ordinances" in v.43?

A: An ordinance is what we call "case law", the application of God's Word in situations which are not specifically, word-for-word addressed in Scripture. It is referring to a believer waiting for illumination from the Holy Spirit where God's Word is concerned in order to convey the right answer in terms of application of God's Word for a particular situation or person.

Q: What is the list of actions which characterize someone who, as specified in v.42, is biblically trusting in God's Word?

- *"I wait"* (v.43)
- *"I will keep"* (v.44)
- *"I will walk"* (v.45)
- *"I will also speak...and not be ashamed"* (v.46)
- *"I shall delight"* (v.47)
- *"I shall lift up my hands"* (v.48)
- *"I will meditate"* (v.48)

---

⁴¹May Your lovingkindnesses also come to me, O LORD,
Your salvation according to Your word;
⁴²So I will have an answer for him who reproaches me,
For I trust in Your word.
⁴³And do not take the word of truth utterly out of my mouth,
For I wait for Your ordinances.
⁴⁴So I will keep Your law continually,
Forever and ever.
⁴⁵And I will walk at liberty,
For I seek Your precepts.
⁴⁶I will also speak of Your testimonies before kings
And shall not be ashamed.
⁴⁷I shall delight in Your commandments,
Which I love.
⁴⁸And I shall lift up my hands to Your commandments,
Which I love;
And I will meditate on Your statutes.

Point: *These provide a cycle covering not only our personal, private relationship with Christ, but our public testimony and witness of Him. At the heart of each one is an aspect of God's Word: "the word of truth", "Your law", "Your precepts", "Your testimonies", "Your commandments" (twice) and "Your statutes".*

Q: What is significant about that which is repeated?
A: *"Your commandments, which I love"* (v.47, 48) is directly connected to the opening verse's identification of *"lovingkindnesses"* (OT term for grace) and *"salvation"*. Biblical commandments are the requirements for a covenant relationship with God.

Application: *The work of salvation can never be separated from the working of God's Word either within us personally or through us to others.*

Overall Application

Q: In each of these examples, what condition is being addressed?

- (v.25-32) God's Word is essential when the heart needs restoration.

- (v.33-40) God's Word is essential when one's spiritual walk needs restoration.

- (v.41-48) God's Word is essential when one's soul needs restoration.

The answer is often not exclusively produced by a prayer request for divine intervention or a supernatural "fix", but often in combination with the Word where they have already been addressed.

Psalm 119 • Master for Handout (#4-6)

1. (v.25-32) **Daleth (ד): A Cure for the Blues.** Obedience to God's Word and ways even when one is **personally** and **emotionally** low provides the appropriate remedy where it matters most: the **heart**.

2. (v.33-40) **He (ה): The Biblical Definition of "Revival"**. Note how these combine to describe a lifestyle of **putting** God's Word into **practice** and not merely obtaining **knowledge**.

3. (v.41-48) **Vav (ו): The Cycle of the Word in the Saved.** The **work** of salvation can never be separated from the **working** of God's Word either **within us** personally or **through us** to others.

For Small Group Leaders to summarize these three lessons:

Overall Application

Q: In each of these examples, what condition is being addressed?

- (v.25-32) God's Word is essential when the **heart** needs restoration.
- v.33-40) God's Word is essential when one's **spiritual walk** needs restoration.
- (v.41-48) God's Word is essential when one's **soul** needs restoration.

The answer is often not exclusively produced by a prayer request for divine **intervention** or a **supernatural** "fix", but often in combination with the Word where they have already been **addressed**.

Psalm 119 Group Handout • Daleth, He & Vav (#4-6)

1. **(v.25-32) Daleth (ד): A Cure for the Blues.** Obedience to God's Word and ways even when one is _____ and _____ low provides the appropriate remedy where it matters most: the _____.

2. **(v.33-40) He (ה): The Biblical Definition of "Revival".** Note how these combine to describe a lifestyle of _____ God's Word into _____ and not merely obtaining _____.

3. **(v.41-48) Vav (ו): The Cycle of the Word in the Saved.** The _____ of salvation can never be separated from the _____ of God's Word either _____ personally or _____ to others.

Overall Application

Q: In each of these examples, what condition is being addressed?

- (v.25-32) God's Word is essential when the _____ needs restoration.
- (v.33-40) God's Word is essential when one's _____ needs restoration.
- (v.41-48) God's Word is essential when one's _____ needs restoration.

The answer is often not exclusively produced by a prayer request for divine _____ or a _____ "fix", but often in combination with the Word where they have already been _____.

Les - Week 3

Psalm 119:49-56, 57-64, 65-72 • Zayin, Heth & Teth (#7-9)

Introduction

[Note: Each stanza of Psalm 119 is a study in and of itself. For the purposes of leading a small group study, these three are presented together as a single study.]

It should not surprise anyone that Psalm 119 is the largest of the 929 chapters in our Bible as it is dedicated to not only explaining how Scripture is organized by its consistent use of 8 categories of God's Word, but repeatedly provides real world examples of how we are to apply every facet of God's Word to our life. The goal is not to determine what we can expect from God's Word, but that which we need to do to meet the personal shortfalls of what God's Word expects from us.

---

⁴⁹Remember the word to Your servant,
In which You have made me hope.
⁵⁰This is my comfort in my affliction,
That Your word has revived me.
⁵¹The arrogant utterly deride me,
Yet I do not turn aside from Your law.
⁵²I have remembered Your ordinances from of old, O LORD,
And comfort myself.
⁵³Burning indignation has seized me because of the wicked,
Who forsake Your law.
⁵⁴Your statutes are my songs In the house of my pilgrimage.
⁵⁵O LORD, I remember Your name in the night,
And keep Your law.
⁵⁶This has become mine,
That I observe Your precepts

[Read v.49-56] Through It All

Q: What are the listed behaviors of those who reject God and His Word?

- (v.51) *"The arrogant utterly deride me..."*
- v.53) *"Burning indignation has seized me because of the wicked, who forsake Your law."* (v.53)

Point: Because the unbelieving express contempt and ridicule for God's Word by forsaking it, they naturally render the same to those who cling to it.

Q: Does this Psalm's author offer that this is something easily dealt with?

A: No, he specifically calls it *"my affliction"*. This is a Hebrew term which describes a state of hardship and trouble.

Q: What does the author do in order to deal with this hardship?

A: *"I...comfort myself"* (v.52) by...

- Remembering God's *"ordinances from old"* (v.52)—that is, the application of His Word in every situation, whether or not it is specifically articulated in Scripture, since the beginning. What He has done, He will continue to do—a continuous action.

80

- Making God's *"statutes...my songs in the house of my pilgrimage"* (v.54)—that is, remaining within the constraints of God's Word, recognizing we are just here temporarily.
- Remembering *"Your name in the night"* (v.55)—that is, obedient to God's Word and ways regardless of the hour or circumstance. The literal darkness of night is often a biblical metaphor for the worst of spiritual conditions.

Application: *Note that neither was a miracle sought to rescue the author personally, nor was God's imprecatory judgment called down to eliminate the source of the affliction. What he seeks is to maintain personal faithfulness to God's Word regardless.*

[Read v.57-64] **My Portion**

Q: What is "portion" referring to? How does it provide an overall context?

> ⁵⁷The Lord is my portion;
> I have promised to keep Your words.
> ⁵⁸I sought Your favor with all my heart;
> Be gracious to me according to Your word.
> ⁵⁹I considered my ways
> And turned my feet to Your testimonies.
> ⁶⁰I hastened and did not delay
> To keep Your commandments.
> ⁶¹The cords of the wicked have encircled me,
> But I have not forgotten Your law.
> ⁶²At midnight I shall rise to give thanks to You
> Because of Your righteous ordinances.
> ⁶³I am a companion of all those who fear You,
> And of those who keep Your precepts.
> ⁶⁴The earth is full of Your lovingkindness, O Lord;
> Teach me Your statutes.

A: This could easily be translated as "inheritance". It is used in Scripture to describe God's people...

"For the LORD'S portion is His people; Jacob is the allotment of His inheritance. (Dt. 32:9)

...and the land of Israel as a literal inheritance for His people...

"Now therefore, apportion this land for an inheritance to the nine tribes and the half-tribe of Manasseh."(Josh. 13:7)

Likewise the believer's inheritance is not actually in the things of this world, but in the Lord as well, an indication of that we are children of the Father, not restricted to being physical descendants of life below.

*... In Him also **we have obtained an inheritance**, having been predestined according to His purpose who works all things after the counsel of His will, to the end that we who were the first to hope in Christ would be to the praise of His glory. (Eph. 1:10a–12)*

*Whatever you do, do your work heartily, as for the Lord rather than for men, knowing that **from the Lord you will receive the reward of the inheritance**. It is the Lord Christ whom you serve.(Col. 3:23–24)*

*Blessed be the God and Father of our Lord Jesus Christ, who according to His great mercy has caused us to be born again to a living hope through the resurrection of Jesus Christ from the dead, **to obtain an inheritance which is imperishable and undefiled and will not fade away, reserved in heaven for you**, who are protected by the power of God through faith for a salvation ready to be revealed in the last time.(1 Pe. 1:3–5)*

Q According to v.58, what is the petitioner seeking for THIS life?
A: "*...Be gracious to me according to Your word*". In other words, he is not asking for supernatural intervention or God's judgment on those aligned against him, but to be treated correspondingly to his degree of faithfulness to God's Word.

Q: What are those things which bode well for the author in this regard where his personal relationship with God is concerned?

- (v.57) "*I have promised to keep Your words*"
- (v.58) "*I sought Your favor*"
- (v.59) "*I...turned my feet to Your testimonies*"
- (v.60) "*I...did not delay to keep Your commandments*"
- (v.61) "*I have not forgotten Your law*"

Q: And where his personal relationships are concerned?
A: "*I am a companion of those who fear You, and of those who keep Your precepts*". (v.63) These are those who not only show the proper respect and reverence for God, but those who have entered into an actual covenant relationship with Him, since a precept can only be obeyed by a believer **AFTER** they have come to faith in God.

Q: What is here indicated that the author's endurance is an additional issue?

A: The reference in v.62 to rising and giving thanks at midnight, something often employed as a spiritual metaphor to speak of the intensity of spiritual issues or an overall spiritual environment.

Q: How do these verses end with a priority for believers where THIS life is concerned?

A: *"Teach me Your statutes"* —that is, the boundaries which God has set for believers designating requirements for them as to how to worship God and pursue biblical relationships, guidelines which allow us to live **IN** the world but **OF** the world..

Application: Believers devoted to God's Word understand that their "portion" or inheritance is not the things of this life, but the next, and always act accordingly in both their heavenly and earthly relationships

[Read v.65-72] The Right Result from Discipline

>⁶⁵You have dealt well with Your servant,
>O LORD, according to Your word.
>⁶⁶Teach me good discernment and knowledge,
>For I believe in Your commandments.
>⁶⁷Before I was afflicted I went astray,
>But now I keep Your word.
>⁶⁸You are good and do good;
>Teach me Your statutes.
>⁶⁹The arrogant have forged a lie against me;
>With all my heart I will observe Your precepts.
>⁷⁰Their heart is covered with fat,
>But I delight in Your law.
>⁷¹It is good for me that I was afflicted,
>That I may learn Your statutes.
>⁷²The law of Your mouth is better to me
>Than thousands of gold and silver pieces.

Q: What is the present situation where the believer is concerned?

A: This is presented in the context of having experienced the discipline of the Lord, and effected the right response to it.

- (v.65) *"You have dealt well with Your servant..."*
- (v.67) *"Before I was afflicted I went astray..."*
- (v.71) *"It is good for me that I was afflicted..."*

Q: What was the right response to the Lord's discipline?

A: *"...but now I keep Your word"*. (v.67) He is no longer just a "hearer" of the Word, but a doer. (Mt. 7:24-27; Ja. 1:23-25)

Q: How is this believer's right response to God's Word contrasted to that of the unbeliever?

A: Not only are unbelievers' identified as *"arrogant"* and manipulating the truth (v.69)—the opposite of the working of God's Word, but the phrase, *"Their heart is covered in fat"* is an idiom used to describe someone who refuses to listen and change.

Q: What are the requested action points now that the backslidden have properly responded to the Lord's discipline?
> A: *"Teach me good discernment and knowledge"* (v.66) in combination with, *"That I may learn".* (v.71) It is far more valuable than anything which can be offered in this life, even a treasure of silver and gold. (v.72)

> ***Application:*** *Faithfulness is the only cure for unfaithfulness, and obedience for disobedience to God's Word and ways.*

Overall Application

Q: How are the first and third lessons ("Zayin" & "Teth") related?
A: The first deals with issues outside our control, the third [*third* written above *second*] with issues which result from within ourselves. It's the difference between a trial and discipline.

Q: How might the second teaching regarding our true inheritance relate?
A: Regardless of what takes place in this life, whether from outside or within, we are never working for the temporal benefits of the world but the eternal of the next life.

Application: *Personal faithfulness to God's Word guides from this life to the next even through the trials the world brings or those we bring on ourselves.*

Psalm 119 • Master for Handout (#7-9)

1. (v.49-56) **Zayin (ז): Through It All**. Note that neither was a **miracle** sought to rescue the author personally, nor was God's **imprecatory judgment** called down to eliminate the source of the affliction. What he seeks is to maintain personal **faithfulness** to God's Word regardless.

2. (v.57-64) **Heth (ח): My Portion**. Believers devoted to God's Word understand that their "portion" or **inheritance** is not the things of **this** life, but the **next**, and always act accordingly in both their heavenly and earthly **relationships**.

3. (v.65-72) **Teth (ט): The Right Result from Discipline**. **Faithfulness** is the only cure for **unfaithfulness**, and **obedience** for **disobedience** to God's Word and ways.

For Small Group Leaders to summarize these three lessons:

Overall Application

Q: How are the first and third lessons ("Zayin" & "Teth") related?
 A: The first deals with issues outside our control, the second with issues which result from within ourselves. It's the difference between a trial and discipline.

Q: How might the second teaching regarding our true inheritance relate?
 A: Regardless of what takes place in this life, whether from outside or within, we are never working for the temporal benefits of the world but the eternal of the next life.

Application: *Personal faithfulness to God's Word guides from this* **life** *to the next even through the trials the* **world** *brings or those we bring on* **ourselves**.

Week 3

Psalm 119 Group Handout • Zayin, Heth & Teth (#7-9)

1. **(v.49-56) Zayin (ז): Through It All.** Note that neither was a _____ sought to rescue the author personally, nor _____ called down to was God's _____ eliminate the source of the affliction. What he seeks is to maintain personal _____ to God's Word regardless.

2. **(v.57-64) Heth (ח): My Portion.** Believers devoted to God's Word understand that their "portion" or _____ is not the things of _____ life, but the _____ and always act accordingly in both their heavenly and earthly _____.

3. **(v.65-72) Teth (ט): The Right Result from Discipline.** _____ is the only cure for _____, and _____ for _____ to God's Word and ways.

Application: Personal faithfulness to God's Word guides from this _____ to the _____ even through the trials the _____ brings or those we bring on _____.

Psalm 119:73-80, 81-88, 89-96 • Yodh, Kaph & Lamedh (#10-12)

Introduction

[Note: Each stanza of Psalm 119 is a study in and of itself. For the purposes of leading a small group study, these three are presented together as a single study.]

It should not surprise anyone that Psalm 119 is the largest of the 929 chapters in our Bible as it is dedicated to not only explaining how Scripture is organized by its consistent use of 8 categories of God's Word, but repeatedly provides real world examples of how we are to apply every facet of God's Word to our life. The goal is not to determine what we can expect from God's Word, but that which we need to do to meet the personal shortfalls of what God's Word expects from us.

> ⁷³Your hands made me and fashioned me;
> Give me understanding, that I may learn Your commandments.
> ⁷⁴May those who fear You see me and be glad,
> Because I wait for Your word.
> ⁷⁵I know, O Lord, that Your judgments are righteous,
> And that in faithfulness You have afflicted me
> ⁷⁶O may Your lovingkindness comfort me,
> According to Your word to Your servant.
> ⁷⁷May Your compassion come to me that I may live,
> For Your law is my delight.
> ⁷⁸May the arrogant be ashamed, for they subvert me with a lie;
> But I shall meditate on Your precepts.
> ⁷⁹May those who fear You turn to me,
> Even those who know Your testimonies.
> ⁸⁰May my heart be blameless in Your statutes,
> So that I will not be ashamed.

[Read v.73-80] A Dual Working in Other

Q: According to v.73, for what purpose were we created?

A: That we should obtain understanding through, and obedience to, God's Word.

Q: In the context of these verses, who are the main targets of a believer's obedience to God's Word?

A: To other believers:

- *"those who fear You"* (v.74 & 79)
- *"those who know Your testimonies"* (v.79)

...and to non-believers:

- *"May the arrogant be ashamed"* (v.76)

Q: What are the attributes of God being emphasized in the course of being an example and witness to both believer and non-believer alike?

A: *"Righteous"* (v.75), *"lovingkindness"* (v.76), and *"compassion"* (v.77). It is an equal application of truth and justice with grace and mercy.

Q: What is the stark difference presented in v.78?

A: Whereas the unsaved *"subvert me with a lie"*, the response is to *"meditate on Your precepts"*, which are those things which only believers put into practice after coming into a personal relationship with God. In other words, the first reaction is not revenge, but self-examination, just as Jesus teaches. (Mt. 7:1-5)

Q: What is the proper result of such a self-examination?
A: According to the closing verse, it is a blameless heart so to avoid the shame of misbehavior to either believers or unbelievers. One's witness remains intact.

Application: *There is a dual working of God's Word through us to build up others in the Body of Christ, and at the same time bear witness to those who have yet to accept Christ as their personal Savior. Our obedience to God's Word and ways simultaneously works on both.*

[Read v.81-88] When Will Justice Come?

Q: What is this believer's spiritual condition according to v.81-82?
A: *"My soul languishes"* (v.81) and *"My eyes fail"*. (v.82)

Q: According to v.83, what is the source of this angst?
A: *"...those who persecute me"*.

Q: What, exactly, are they doing?
A: *"The arrogant have dug pits for me"* (v.85)—the way of describing in that time and culture traps being set.

Q: How do we know that this is speaking of traps of a spiritual nature?
A: Because in the same verse they are described as, *"Men who are not in accord with Your law"*, meaning they are operating outside and against it. This is further verified in v.86 when their persecution is identified in the form of *"a lie"*.

Q: Does the author ask for supernatural intervention or imprecatory judgment upon his persecutors?
A: Although *"They almost destroyed me on earth"*, (v.87) what is requested is be sustained as a faithful example of God's precepts—that which is required of believer's alone, and His testimony—both the consequences and benefits of His Word as stated by God personally.

Application: *Persecution of believers has always resulted in not just refining and strengthening the faith and walk of believer's, but in having a multiplying effectiveness where the opportunities to share the Gospel with unbelievers is*

---

⁸¹My soul languishes for Your salvation;
I wait for Your word.
⁸²My eyes fail with longing for Your word,
While I say, "When will You comfort me?"
⁸³Though I have become like a wineskin in the smoke,
I do not forget Your statutes.
⁸⁴How many are the days of Your servant?
When will You execute judgment on those who persecute me?
⁸⁵The arrogant have dug pits for me,
Men who are not in accord with Your law.
⁸⁶All Your commandments are faithful;
They have persecuted me with a lie; help me!
⁸⁷They almost destroyed me on earth,
But as for me, I did not forsake Your precepts.
⁸⁸Revive me according to Your lovingkindness,
So that I may keep the testimony of Your mouth.

concerned. There is unlimited time in eternity for justice, but only a short window in this life to avoid it.

[Read v.89-96] Eternal Protection

Q: What might be a very daunting contrast and comparison in these verses?

A: The eternal faithfulness of God's Word extending both into eternity past and future (v.89-90) and our absolute dependence on it to first revive and sustain us.

Q: Why might the latter half of v.91 be telling us about an aspect of God's greater plan where we are concerned?

A: The reference to, *"For all things are Your servants"* indicates that His intention for Creation is the same for us, that everything is created to ultimately worship and serve Him.

Q: Therefore, how does the believer personally proceed where God's Word is concerned?

A: He commits to it in every conceivable way because *"Your word is settled in heaven"*, (v.89) whereas when it comes to the temporal things of this life, *"I have seen a limit to all perfection"*. (v.96)

Q: How does this contrast to both our personal nature's working on earth and that of unbelievers?

A: Left to our own devices, we would perish in our affliction (v.92) having never recovered from it through God's Word (v.93), and if left up to *"the wicked"*—those willfully acting contrarily to God's Word and ways, they would destroy us.

Q: What is the closing verse describing?

A: The Hebrew word *"broad"* is being contrasted with that of *"limit"*. It is a way of stating that earthly perfection is finite and can only extend so far, but God's Word is limitless.

Application: *In this life we have the choice of obedience to the eternal nature of God's Word, which not only established Creation and extends to eternity past, but to our eternity future, or remain with the limitations of earthly perfection, which is actually no perfection at all.*

---

⁸⁹Forever, O LORD,
Your word is settled in heaven.
⁹⁰Your faithfulness continues throughout all generations;
You established the earth, and it stands.
⁹¹They stand this day according to Your ordinances,
For all things are Your servants.
⁹²If Your law had not been my delight,
Then I would have perished in my affliction.
⁹³I will never forget Your precepts,
For by them You have revived me.
⁹⁴I am Yours, save me;
For I have sought Your precepts.
⁹⁵The wicked wait for me to destroy me;
I shall diligently consider Your testimonies.
⁹⁶I have seen a limit to all perfection;
Your commandment

Overall Application

Q: What appears to be a common, underlying theme in these teachings?
    A: The contrast of the temporal—this life, and the eternal—the next life.

Q: Why do things in this life matter where eternity is concerned? Aren't we all destined for death anyway?
    A: Our soul is actually immortal and will not cease just because our life on this planet ends.

<u>Application</u> How we live here determines where we live there. And as it turns out, it's not just how we live individually in and of ourselves, but how we live with others.

Psalm 119 • Master for Handout (#10-12)

1. (v.73-80) **Yodh (י): A Dual Working in Others.** There is a **dual** working of God's Word through us to build up others in the Body of Christ, and at the same time **bear witness** to those who have yet to accept Christ as their personal Savior. Our obedience to God's Word and ways simultaneously **works** on **both**.

2. (v.81-88) **Kaph (כ): When Will Justice Come?** Persecution of believers has always resulted in not just refining and strengthening the faith and walk of **believer's**, but in having a multiplying effectiveness where the opportunities to share the Gospel with **unbelievers** is concerned. There is unlimited time in **eternity** for justice, but only a short window in **this life** to avoid it.

3. (v.89-96) **Lamedh (ל): Eternal Perfection.** In this life we have the choice of obedience to the **eternal** nature of God's Word, which not only established Creation and extends to **eternity** past, but to our eternity future, or remain with the limitations of earthly **perfection**, which is actually no **perfection** at all.

For Small Group Leaders to summarize these three lessons:

Overall Application

Q: **What appears to be a common, underlying theme in these teachings?**
   A: The contrast of the temporal—this life, and the eternal—the next life.

Q: **Why do things in this life matter where eternity is concerned? Aren't we all destined for death anyway?**
   A: Our soul is actually immortal and will not cease just because our life on this planet ends.

Application How we live **here** determines where we live **there**. And as it turns out, it's not just how we live **individually** in and of ourselves, but how we live with **others**.

Psalm 119 Group Handout • Yodh, Kaph & Lamedh (#10-12)

1. **v.73-80) Yodh (י): A Dual Working in Others.** There is a _____ working of God's Word through us to _____ others in the Body of Christ, and at the same time _____ to those who have yet to accept Christ as their personal Savior. Our obedience to God's Word and ways simultaneously _____ on _____.

2. **v.81-88) Kaph (כ): When Will Justice Come?** Persecution of believers has always resulted in not just refining and strengthening the faith and walk of _____, but in having a multiplying effectiveness where the opportunities to share the Gospel with _____ is concerned. There is unlimited time in _____ for justice, but only a short window in _____ to avoid it.

3. **(v.89-96) Lamedh (ל): Eternal Perfection.** In this life we have the choice of obedience to the _____ nature of God's Word, which not only established Creation and extends to _____ past, but to our _____ future, or remain with the limitations of earthly _____, which is actually no _____ at all.

Application: *How we live _____ determines where we live _____. And as it turns out, it's not just how we live _____ in and of ourselves, but how we live with _____*

Simon/Kathy 9/11/22

Psalm 119:97-104, 105-112, 113-120 • Mem, Nun & Samekh (#13-15)

Introduction

God's word makes us wise - wiser than our enemies & wiser than any teachers who ignore it. True wisdom goes beyond amassing knowledge, it is applying knowledge in a life changing way. Intelligent or experienced people are not necessarily wise. Wisdom comes from allowing what God teaches us to guide us.

Note: Each stanza of Psalm 119 is a study in and of itself. For the purposes of leading a small group study, these three are presented together as a single study.]

It should not surprise anyone that Psalm 119 is the largest of the 929 chapters in our Bible as it is dedicated to not only explaining how Scripture is organized by its consistent use of 8 categories of God's Word, but repeatedly provides real world examples of how we are to apply every facet of God's Word to our life. The goal is not to determine what we can expect from God's Word, but that which we need to do to meet the personal shortfalls of what God's Word expects from us.

> ¹²¹I have done justice and righteousness;
> Do not leave me to my oppressors.
> ¹²²Be surety for Your servant for good;
> Do not let the arrogant oppress me.
> ¹²³My eyes fail with longing for Your salvation
> And for Your righteous word.
> ¹²⁴Deal with Your servant according to Your lovingkindness
> And teach me Your statutes.
> ¹²⁵I am Your servant; give me understanding,
> That I may know Your testimonies.
> ¹²⁶It is time for the LORD to act,
> For they have broken Your law.
> ¹²⁷Therefore I love Your commandments
> Above gold, yes, above fine gold.
> ¹²⁸Therefore I esteem right all Your precepts concerning everything,
> I hate every false way.

[Read v.97-104] The Power of Meditation

Q: What is the key action where our approach to God's Word is concerned, which is repeated twice in these verses?

A: *"Meditation"*. (v. 97, 99) It is incorporating God's Word into our prayer life so that they are inseparable.

Observation: Scripture rarely advises us to simply "read" God's Word; the two most often used commands are to "study" and "meditate". This is because while prayer is the way **WE** talk to God, His Word is the way He most often talks to **US**. Without incorporating the Word in this way, prayer is a one-way conversation.

Q: How would meditating on God's commandments (v,98) make one "wiser than my enemies"?

A: By definition a commandment is a requirement for someone who has entered into a covenant relationship with God. Therefore, by default, a believer's enemies are in a relationship with Satan, something which can be characterized even beyond just being unwise.

Q: How would meditating on God's testimonies (v.99) provide "more insight than all my teachers"?
> A: By definition a testimony is God personally bearing witness to the benefits and/or consequences of obedience or disobedience where His Word is concerned. It is addressing the necessary issue that we pay more attention to God than man, even if our teachers are likewise believers.

Q: How would meditating on God's precepts (v.100) provide understanding "more than the aged"? *ie. what tru*
> A: By definition a precept is something required after a person enters into a covenant relationship with Christ. It is addressing the fervor with which one pursues their personal sanctification as it relates to obedience to His Word and ways, something a long-time believer has been engaged in longer than most. But even new believers can accelerate their growth by their obedience to His Word.

Q: How do v.101 & 102 describe additional requirements on our part where our personal behavior is concerned?
> A: "I have restrained my feet from every evil way" is a proactive stance against personal sin, combined with doing so consistently as indicated by, "I have not turned aside". It is avoiding part-time obedience to engage in full-time obedience.

Q: What might be a surprising benefit according to v.103?
> A: It is both enjoyable and refreshing to be in such a lifestyle.

Q: How does this ultimately change our attitude and behavior?
> A: Instead of entertaining the notion of, and sometimes pursuing, false ways, we come to hate them, and actively avoid them.

Application: *This all comports to the theme of meditating on God's Word, meaning that it is not just never out of our thoughts, but that we can no longer even entertain an alternative to first and foremost obey it.*

> ¹²⁹Your testimonies are wonderful;
> Therefore my soul observes them.
> ¹³⁰The unfolding of Your words gives light;
> It gives understanding to the simple.
> ¹³¹I opened my mouth wide and panted,
> For I longed for Your commandments.
> ¹³²Turn to me and be gracious to me,
> After Your manner with those who love Your name.
> ¹³³Establish my footsteps in Your word,
> And do not let any iniquity have dominion over me.
> ¹³⁴Redeem me from the oppression of man,
> That I may keep Your precepts.
> ¹³⁵Make Your face shine upon Your servant,
> And teach me Your statutes.
> ¹³⁶My eyes shed streams of water,
> Because they do not keep Your law.

[Read v.105-112] The Light of the Word

Q: In the context of these verses, why is the lamp of God's Word so badly needed where the world is concerned?
A: "*I am exceedingly afflicted*" (v.107) and "*The wicked have laid a snare for me*". (v.110) In times of spiritual darkness, we are even more dependent on the light of God's Word to illuminate the sole path to which we need to cling.

Q: But how does v.109 identify an additional threat?
A: "*My life is continually in my hand*" indicates freewill and choice, and the ever-present danger of making a personal decision contrary to God's Word and ways.

Q: How are "the wicked" trying to take advantage of this?
A: By laying "*a snare*", (v.110) something intended to take us away from the Lord. The remedy is to not go astray from God's Word, particularly in the case of His precepts, those things which are specifically required of a believer maintaining a right relationship with God.

Q: What is the believer's inheritance which matters in this life?
A: "*Your testimonies forever*". (v.111) For believers this is God's assurance of the benefits of obedience to His Word, and to the wicked the assurance of the consequences for disobedience.

Q: What is the kind of commitment to obedience which is required when it comes to God's Word?
A: "*Forever, even to the end*". (v.112) We are to never turn back.

Application: *God's Word will always provide enough illumination to allow us to keep to the proper path. As Jesus IS the Word, we can see why, in eternity, there is no need for any other Light.*

> *And the city has no need of the sun or of the moon to shine on it, for the glory of God has illumined it, and its lamp is the Lamb.* — Revelation 21:23

Double Minded

> ¹³⁷Righteous are You, O LORD,
> And upright are Your judgments.
> ¹³⁸You have commanded Your testimonies in righteousness
> And exceeding faithfulness.
> ¹³⁹My zeal has consumed me,
> Because my adversaries have forgotten Your words.
> ¹⁴⁰Your word is very pure,
> Therefore Your servant loves it.
> ¹⁴¹I am small and despised,
> Yet I do not forget Your precepts.
> ¹⁴²Your righteousness is an everlasting righteousness,
> And Your law is truth.
> ¹⁴³Trouble and anguish have come upon me,
> Yet Your commandments are my delight.
> ¹⁴⁴Your testimonies are righteous forever;
> Give me understanding that I may live.

[Read v.113-120] The Right Response

Q: What are the four types of non-believers identified and what do they all have in common?

A: They are the "*double-minded*" (v.113), "*evildoers*" (v.115), "*those who wander*". (v.118), and "*the wicked*" (v.119) They are all different types of straying from God's Word.

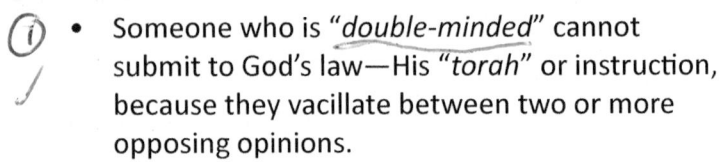

① • Someone who is "*double-minded*" cannot submit to God's law—His "*torah*" or instruction, because they vacillate between two or more opposing opinions.

> *Elijah came near to all the people and said, "How long will you hesitate between two opinions? If the LORD is God, follow Him; but if Baal, follow him." But the people did not answer him a word. (1 Kings 18:21)*

② • An "*evildoer*" acts in direct contradiction to God's Word and ways and actively pursues an entirely opposite manner from God's Word.

③ • Someone who wanders is not making a commitment to anything, much less God.

④ • And the "*wicked*" are ultimately removed because they are the active agents of Satan and sin.

Q: What is the most significant contrast between the believer and these types of non-believers as articulated in v.120?

A: The believer in THIS life fears God ("*my flesh trembles for fear of You*"), knowing from His "case law"("*Your judgments*") that there are no loopholes.

Observation: *It is interesting to note that in the Gospels, Jesus spends far more time and energy warning about hell than speaking about heaven.*

Q: While these various types of non-believers attempt their shenanigans, what is the appropriate response for the believer?

v114

- (v.114) "*You are my hiding place*"
- (v.114) "*...and my shield*"
- (v.114) "*I wait for Your word*"

Application: *The right response to the total spectrum of non-believers is God's Word. It hides us, protects us, and always comes at the appropriate time.*

> *So will My word be which goes forth from My mouth; It will not return to Me empty, Without accomplishing what I desire, And without succeeding in the matter for which I sent it. (Isaiah 55:11)*

Psalm 119 • Handout for Master (#13-15)

1. (v.97-104) **Mem (מ): The Power of Meditation**. This all comports to the theme of **meditating** on God's Word, meaning that it is not just never out of our **thoughts**, but that we can no longer even entertain an **alternative** to first and foremost obey it.

2. (v.105-112) **Nun (נ): The Light of the Word**. God's Word will always provide enough **illumination** to allow us to keep to the proper path. As Jesus IS the Word, we can see why, in **eternity**, there is no need for any other **Light**.

3. (v.113-120) **Samekh (ס): The Right Response**. The right response to the total spectrum of **non-believers** is God's Word. It **hides** us, **protects** us, and always comes at the appropriate **time**.

For Small Group Leaders to summarize these three lessons:

Overall Application

Q: What is the difference between "reading" and "meditating"?
A: "Reading" is an informational approach, but "meditating" is incarnational—that is, the process by which God's Word becomes a part of us.

Q: How might that be important when it comes the working of the Word as our light?
A: Whereas an informational approach may show something about God's path, when the Word becomes a part of us we do not allow ourselves to stray from the path—we follow up with obedience.

Q: How might these teachings actually successively lead into each other?

- We incorporate God's Word into our **prayer** life.
- God's Word **illuminates** our way.
- God's Word works in us **personally** and as a visible **witness**.

Psalm 119 Group Handout • Mem, Nun & Samekh (#13-15)

1. **(v.97-104) Mem (מ): The Power of Meditation.** This all comports to the theme of _____ on God's Word, meaning that it is not just never out of our _____, but that we can no longer even entertain an _____ to first and foremost obey it.

2. **(v.105-112) Nun (נ): The Light of the Word.** God's Word will always provide enough _____ to allow us to keep to the proper path. As Jesus IS the Word, we can see why, in _____, there is no need for any other _____.

- **(v.113-120) Samekh (ס): The Right Response.** The right response to the total spectrum of _____ is God's Word. It _____ us, _____ us, and always comes at the appropriate _____.

Overall Application

Q: How might these teachings actually successively lead into each other?

- We incorporate God's Word into our _____ life.
- God's Word _____ our way.
- God's Word works in us _____ and as a visible _____.

Psalm 119:121-128, 129-136, 137-144 • Ayin, Pe & Tsadhe (#16-18)

Introduction

[Note: Each stanza of Psalm 119 is a study in and of itself. For the purposes of leading a small group study, these three are presented together as a single study.]

It should not surprise anyone that Psalm 119 is the largest of the 929 chapters in our Bible as it is dedicated to not only explaining how Scripture is organized by its consistent use of 8 categories of God's Word, but repeatedly provides real world examples of how we are to apply every facet of God's Word to our life. The goal is not to determine what we can expect from God's Word, but that which we need to do to meet the personal shortfalls of what God's Word expects from us.

> ¹²¹I have done justice and righteousness;
> Do not leave me to my oppressors.
> ¹²²Be surety for Your servant for good;
> Do not let the arrogant oppress me.
> ¹²³My eyes fail with longing for Your salvation
> And for Your righteous word.
> ¹²⁴Deal with Your servant according to Your lovingkindness
> And teach me Your statutes.
> ¹²⁵I am Your servant; give me understanding,
> That I may know Your testimonies.
> ¹²⁶It is time for the LORD to act,
> For they have broken Your law.
> ¹²⁷Therefore I love Your commandments
> Above gold, yes, above fine gold.
> ¹²⁸Therefore I esteem right all Your precepts concerning everything,
> I hate every false way.

[Read v.121-128] I Am Your Servant

Q: What is the nature of the situation being addressed?
   A: Persecution or conflict being inflicted by others.

- (v.121) *"...Do not leave me to my oppressors."*
- (v.122) *"...Do not let the arrogant oppress me."*

Q: What are these oppressors specifically called? How does this reflect their attitude when it comes to God's Word?
   A: They are called *"arrogant"* (v.122) and *"they have broken Your law"*. (v.126) They either think they know better, or above God's Word, or both.

Q: How does this serve as the basis for how the writer of this Psalm presents himself in contrast to the opposition's behavior?
   A: He has a completely different regard and practice where God's Word is concerned:

- (v.122) *"My eyes fail with longing...for Your righteous word."*
- (v.127) *"...I love Your commandments..."*
- (v.128) *"I esteem right all Your precepts..."*
- (v.128) *"...I hate every false way."*

Application: *In other words, he is the opposite of someone characterized as arrogant and a law breaker in terms of his own personal treatment of God's Word. How would we fare in a similar comparison?*

Q: In the believer's statement of longing for salvation, what are the accompanying requests which work towards that goal?

- (v.124) *"...teach me Your statutes"*. These are limitations placed on believers for their own good. In this case, they stand in stark contrast to *"the arrogant"* (v.22) who *"have broken Your law"*. (v.126)
- (v.125) *"...give me understanding, that I may know Your testimonies"*. These are God's personal responses on the benefits and consequences of His Word and contrast the pursuit of *"every false way"* (v.128) which characterizes their overall behavior.

Application: *God's Word provides the believer insight not only into what God is doing in their personal life and situation, but into the root causes of those working in opposition to the believer. God's Word is a dual-edged sword cutting in opposite directions for each based on the condition of their heart, the believer for comfort and understanding, the non-believer for condemnation and judgment.*

Q: What might be interesting about the request, "It is time for the Lord to act"? What is the justification, and what specific actions are being requested?

A: The justification is, *"For they have broken Your law"* (v.126), but all of the requests have to do with requests for God to provide the believer a deeper understanding of the different aspects of His Word. There is never a request for something specific to happen to the non-believers, that being left solely to God's discretion.

Application: *Even when it comes to non-believers, the primary concern is still God's Word.*

Q: What are the labels presented in the course of these verses which best provide insight into the fundamental difference between the one following God's Word and ways versus the one who is not?

A: *"I am your servant"* (v.125) versus *"the arrogant"* (v.122). A Scripture-practicing believer is always first and foremost concerned about his own personal compliance with God's Word which results in a subservient relationship to Christ.

Application: *When a believer is actively opposed by others, the right response is to run back to God's Word. Even when completely justified by one's personal obedience so as to be the total innocent victim of oppression, it is not only left up to God to act according to His will, but seen as yet another opportunity to gain greater personal insight into His Word and ways.*

[Read v.129-136] The Power of the Name

Q: What are the specific personal traits of someone who truly puts God's Word into practice?

> ¹²⁹Your testimonies are wonderful;
> Therefore my soul observes them.
> ¹³⁰The unfolding of Your words gives light;
> It gives understanding to the simple.
> ¹³¹I opened my mouth wide and panted,
> For I longed for Your commandments.
> ¹³²Turn to me and be gracious to me,
> After Your manner with those who love Your name.
> ¹³³Establish my footsteps in Your word,
> And do not let any iniquity have dominion over me.
> ¹³⁴Redeem me from the oppression of man,
> That I may keep Your precepts.
> ¹³⁵Make Your face shine upon Your servant,
> And teach me Your statutes.
> ¹³⁶My eyes shed streams of water,
> Because they do not keep Your law.

- (v.131) *"I opened my mouth wide and panted, for I longed for Your commandments."* They do not merely view God's Word as leading to or describing life, but a vital integral part OF their life.

- (v.132) They *"love Your name"*—that is, their obedience stems from not simply following instructions, but motivated by personal love. An example is when David confessed, *"Against You, You only I have sinned"* (Ps. 51:4); where God's Word is concerned it is extremely personal.

- (v.136) *"My eyes shed streams of water, because they do not keep Your law."* Having personally established themselves in God's Word and ways, they experience an equally personal burden for those who have not.

Q: What is contained in v.132-135 which identifies the nature of what the writer is asking God to do where these qualities are concerned?

- (v.132) The writer begins by requesting treatment which begins with an examination of his own, personal faithfulness, and not for an exemption because of the lack of it.

- (v.133) This is a way of stating that the way to avoid sin's undue influence is by sticking to God's path alone. In NT terms we call this the process of "sanctification".

- (v.134) The writer does not request action against *"the oppression of man"* except that it go hand-in-hand with the opportunity, *"That I may keep Your precepts"*. It is an opportunity for personal witness where the working of God's Word is concerned.

- (v.135) The favor of God sought in this life is characterized as someone who is teachable when it comes to God's Word.

Q: Why is it specified, "those who love Your name"? Why doesn't it state, "those who love You" to make it even more personal?

A: This is most likely another allusion to the importance of God's Word in the believer's life. A great many names for the members of the Godhead are provided in both Testaments, each provided in order to teach about important attributes. God is so vastly big, and yet His Word allows us to know Him personally through each of His names, teaching us what He is truly like. All of these attributes combine to teach about the inherent power in His name.

Application: *When we study in detail each of the names of God rather than just reading them, we not only acquire knowledge about His working and character, but it actually provides a foundation for why we love Him.*

Q: What is fundamentally different about Christ's name, for instance, from our own? How is it more than just a label?

A: The name of Christ actually has power and produces tangible results, unlike every other name which cannot result in anything.

*Or do you not know that the unrighteous will not inherit the kingdom of God? Do not be deceived; neither fornicators, nor idolaters, nor adulterers, nor effeminate, nor homosexuals, nor thieves, nor the covetous, nor drunkards, nor revilers, nor swindlers, will inherit the kingdom of God. Such were some of you; but you were washed, but you were sanctified, but you were justified **in the name of the Lord Jesus Christ and in the Spirit of our God**. (1 Co. 6:9-11)*

Application: A personal relationship characterized by biblical love with Christ is not just defined by our deep emotional and spiritual attachment to Christ personally, but it results in our deep concern for others who are not experiencing the same. We understand that it is not just the eternal consequences they will experience in the next life, but the benefits and blessings they are foregoing in this one.

[Read v.137-144] The True Working of Righteousness

> ¹³⁷Righteous are You, O LORD,
> And upright are Your judgments.
> ¹³⁸You have commanded Your testimonies in righteousness
> And exceeding faithfulness.
> ¹³⁹My zeal has consumed me,
> Because my adversaries have forgotten Your words.
> ¹⁴⁰Your word is very pure,
> Therefore Your servant loves it.
> ¹⁴¹I am small and despised,
> Yet I do not forget Your precepts.
> ¹⁴²Your righteousness is an everlasting righteousness,
> And Your law is truth.
> ¹⁴³Trouble and anguish have come upon me,
> Yet Your commandments are my delight.
> ¹⁴⁴Your testimonies are righteous forever;
> Give me understanding that I may live.

Q: Based on its repeated usage in this passage, what is the main theme of this teaching?
　　A: *"Righteousness"*. (v.137, 138, 142, & 144) An additional related term is *"upright"*. (v.137)

Q: What are some of the accompanying descriptions of God's Word which go hand-in-hand with the quality of righteousness?

- (v.138) *"...exceeding faithfulness"*—that is, consistent in its adherence to God's Word and ways.
- (v.140) *"...very pure"*—that is, unpolluted by sin.
- (v.142) *"...an everlasting righteousness"*—that is, it is not temporal but stands from eternity past to eternity future.

Q: What are the personal issues which the writer provides insight, things with which he is struggling?
　　A: *"I am small and despised"* (v.141) and *"Trouble and anguish have come upon me"*. (v.143)

Q: But how does he deal with them?
> A: "...yet I do not forget Your precepts" (v.141) and "...yet Your commandments are my delight". (v.143) Regardless of the circumstances, he is still obedient to the biblical requirements for a covenant relationship with God ("*commandments*") and God's requirements after such a commitment ("*precepts*").

Application: *When we find ourselves in similar situations, how often do we run to God's Word rather than put all our effort into praying a way out of the situation? Have you noticed how the words "prayer" and "pray" are seldom featured in Psalm 119? Why do you suppose that is? Consider the old saying, "Prayer is how we talk to God, His Word is how He answers us".*

Q: How is this a major difference when it comes to those who follow His Word and those who do not?
> A: "My zeal has consumed me, because my adversaries have forgotten Your words". (v.139) It is the dual aspect that opponents disregard God's Word and live according to something else in its place, most often working and behaving in direct opposition, and in spite of what takes place; the practitioner, however, never steers away from obedience and compliance.

Q: What is probably the greater meaning in the closing request, "Give me understanding that I may live"?
> A: The true biblical definition of "life" is to begin living now in accordance with God's Word and ways so that we may ensure eternal life; it is not to automatically seek comfort and security in the temporal years on this planet which is in general referred to as "life". Obedience to His Word allows us to live both now and in eternity to come.

Application: *No situation abrogates not just the requirements, but the greater personal need, for obedience to God's Word and ways. This is the working of righteousness where the believer is concerned.*

Overall Application

Q: In whom is the Word working in these three examples?
   A: The primary conduit is the believer, but if applied correctly, it works through them in others, in this case both the unsaved and even outright personal enemies.

Q: So what is the visible evidence of the working of righteousness in the individual believer?
   A: The world—that is, others—will be treated in accordance with God's Word and ways.
   Application: The proof that we are obedient to God's Word internally is clearly revealed by our treatment of others externally.

<u>Application:</u> *The proof that we are obedient to God's Word internally is clearly revealed by our treatment of others externally.*

Psalm 119 • Master for Handout (#16-18)

1. **(v.121-128) Ayin (ע): I Am Your Servant.** When a believer is actively **opposed** by others, the right response is to run back to God's Word. Even when completely justified by one's personal obedience so as to be the total **innocent victim** of oppression, it is not only left up to God to act according to His **will**, but seen as yet another opportunity to gain greater personal **insight** into His Word and ways.

2. **(v.129-136) Pe (פ): The Power of the Name.** A personal relationship characterized by biblical **love** with Christ is not just defined by our deep emotional and spiritual **attachment** to Christ personally, but it results in our deep **concern** for others who are not experiencing the same. We understand that it is not just the eternal **consequences** they will experience in the next life, but the **benefits** and **blessings** they are foregoing in this one.

3. **(v.137-144) Tsadhe (צ): The True Working of Righteousness.** No situation abrogates not just the **requirements**, but the greater personal **need**, for obedience to God's Word and ways. This is the working of **righteousness** where the believer is concerned.

For Small Group Leaders to summarize these three lessons:

Overall Application

Q: In whom is the Word working in these three examples?
A: The primary conduit is the believer, but if applied correctly, it works through them in others, in this case both the unsaved and even outright personal enemies.

Q: So what is the visible evidence of the working of righteousness in the individual believer?
A: The world—that is, others—will be treated in accordance with God's Word and ways.

Application: The proof that we are obedient to God's Word internally is clearly revealed by our treatment of others externally.

Psalm 119 Group Handout • Ayin, Pe & Tsadhe (#16-18)

1. **(v.121-128) Ayin (ע): I Am Your Servant.** When a believer is actively _____ by others, the right response is to run back to God's Word. Even when completely justified by one's personal obedience so as to be the total _____ of oppression, it is not only left up to God to act according to His _____, but seen as yet another opportunity to gain greater personal _____ into His Word and ways.

2. **(v.129-136) Pe (פ): The Power of the Name.** A personal relationship characterized by biblical _____ with Christ is not just defined by our deep emotional and spiritual _____ to Christ personally, but it results in our deep _____ for others who are not experiencing the same. We understand that it is not just the eternal _____ they will experience in the next life, but the _____ and _____ they are foregoing in this one.

3. **(v.137-144) Tsadhe (צ): The True Working of Righteousness.** No situation abrogates not just the _____, but the greater personal _____, for obedience to God's Word and ways. This is the working of _____ where the believer is concerned.

Application: *The proof that we are obedient to God's Word _____ is clearly revealed by our treatment of others _____.*

Psalm 119: 145-152, 153-160 • Qoph & Resh (#19-20)

Introduction

[Note: Each stanza of Psalm 119 is a study in and of itself. For the purposes of leading a small group study, these three are presented together as a single study.]

It should not surprise anyone that Psalm 119 is the largest of the 929 chapters in our Bible as it is dedicated to not only explaining how Scripture is organized by its consistent use of 8 categories of God's Word, but repeatedly provides real world examples of how we are to apply every facet of God's Word to our life. The goal is not to determine what we can expect from God's Word, but that which we need to do to meet the personal shortfalls of what God's Word expects from us.

> ¹⁴⁵I cried with all my heart; answer me, O LORD!
> I will observe Your statutes.
> ¹⁴⁶I cried to You; save me
> And I shall keep Your testimonies.
> ¹⁴⁷I rise before dawn and cry for help;
> I wait for Your words.
> ¹⁴⁸My eyes anticipate the night watches,
> That I may meditate on Your word.
> ¹⁴⁹Hear my voice according to Your lovingkindness;
> Revive me, O LORD, according to Your ordinances.
> ¹⁵⁰Those who follow after wickedness draw near;
> They are far from Your law.
> ¹⁵¹You are near, O LORD,
> And all Your commandments are truth.
> ¹⁵²Of old I have known from Your testimonies
> That You have founded them forever.

[Read v.145-152] In the Meantime

Q: In these opening verses, what is the list of actions which the writer has taken?

- (v.145) *"I cried with all my heart, answer me, O LORD!"*
- (v.146) *"I cried to You, save me..."*
- (v.147) *"I rise before dawn and cry for help..."*

Q: What seems to be the cause of this angst?
A: *"Those who follow after wickedness draw near"*. (v.150) It is not just an issue of dealing with those who may not believe, but those whose personal behavior and practices are completely opposed to those established by God's Word and ways, what is meant by their pursuing *"wickedness"*.

Q: How would this relate to the assertion, "My eyes anticipate the night watches"? (v.148)
A: It is a way of stating that he has been looking for and waiting for an answer around the clock, not just temporarily engaged. It is a poetic way of describing both patience and endurance.

Q: But in the meantime, what has been and continues to be his response?

- (v.145) *"...I will **observe** Your statutes"*.
- (v.146) *"...I shall **keep** Your testimonies"*.
- (v.147) *"...I **wait** for Your words"*.
- (v.148) *"...I...**meditate** on Your word"*.

110

Q: In what context does the writer expect the response will come?

- (v.149) *"Hear my voice according to Your lovingkindness"*. It is first and foremost a response rooted in God's grace and mercy.

- (v.149) *"Revive me, O Lord, according to Your ordinances"*. He will find that he has properly applied God's Word (the meaning of "ordinances") to his particular situation by remaining faithful to the Word through the entire situation, even while awaiting a final response.

- (v.152) *"Of old I have known from Your testimonies that You have founded them [Your commandments] forever."* Faith in the foundation of God's Word serves to justify our need for His Word to be equally enforced in the present circumstances.

Q: What might be ironic about the statement in v.150? How does it contrast to the writer's own situation?

A: Because of non-compliance with God's Word, the wicked are *"far from Your law"*. But while in this case the petitioner feels his own distance from God, he is actually drawn close because of consistent faithfulness to His Word even in the absence of a definitive resolution by earthly standards. In spiritual things as well as earthly, appearances can be deceiving.

Application: *What is the correct response to every earthly situation where God's Word is concerned?*

> ¹⁵³Look upon my affliction and rescue me,
> For I do not forget Your law.
> ¹⁵⁴Plead my cause and redeem me;
> Revive me according to Your word.
> ¹⁵⁵Salvation is far from the wicked,
> For they do not seek Your statutes.
> ¹⁵⁶Great are Your mercies, O LORD;
> Revive me according to Your ordinances.
> ¹⁵⁷Many are my persecutors and my adversaries,
> Yet I do not turn aside from Your testimonies.
> ¹⁵⁸I behold the treacherous and loathe them,
> Because they do not keep Your word.
> ¹⁵⁹Consider how I love Your precepts;
> Revive me, O LORD, according to Your lovingkindness.
> ¹⁶⁰The sum of Your word is truth,
> And every one of Your righteous ordinances is everlasting.

[Read v.153-160] Revive Me

Q: What is the repeated request which provides the overall context? How is this to be accomplished?

- (v.154) "...***Revive me*** according to Your word". [*Redeem me*]
- (v.156) "...***Revive me*** according to Your ordinances". [*Preserve me*]
- (v.159) "...***Revive me***, O LORD, according to Your lovingkindness" as resulting from, "Consider how I love Your precepts". [*Preserve me*]

Application: *When seeking a personal revival or restoration, these are probably the three most important aspects of God's Word—"Your word", "Your ordinances" and "Your precepts", because they are not revisiting the basic requirements of a covenant relationship, but addressing the deeper aspects which come after. They are foundational to a continuing and deepening relationship, whereas "commandments" and "law" are the entry level requirements. We have already "entered" once, the issue is now returning to what we already know and continuing in faithfulness to what subsequently follows.*

Q: What is requested as part of the overall process to be revived?

- (v.153) *"Look upon my affliction and rescue me..."*
- (v.154) *"Plead my cause and redeem me..."*

The request is for Christ our Advocate to *"rescue"* and *"redeem"*, terms Scripture often associates with salvation.

> *"Even now, behold, my witness is in heaven,*
> *And **my advocate is on high**. — Job 16:19*

> *My little children, I am writing these things to you so that you may not sin. And if anyone sins, **we have an Advocate with the Father, Jesus Christ the righteous**; and He Himself is the propitiation for our sins; and not for ours only, but also for those of the whole world. — 1 John 2:1–2*

Q: Is there an indication in the text of how salvation relates to both the righteous and the wicked?
> A: *"Salvation is far from the wicked, for they do not seek Your statutes"*. (v.155) Obedience to God's Word and ways is directly connected to both.

Q: Is a source for his "affliction" (v.153) and need for the Lord to "Plead my cause" (v.154) provided?
> A: In v.157 they are specifically identified as *"my persecutors and my adversaries"*. They are coming from earthly antagonists.

Q: In this situation, how does he personally respond while awaiting God's resolution to these things?
> A: *"…Yet I do not turn aside from Your testimonies"*. (v.157) In spite of the circumstances, the chief response is to faithfully keep God's Word.

Q: Why is this especially a difficult thing to do?
> A: *"I behold the treacherous and loathe them, because they do not keep Your word"*. (v.158) They are not only refusing to adhere to the same standard where God's Word is concerned, but they engage in the perversion of their own word by means of perpetrating treachery, a Hebrew word which is closely aligned with the meaning of deceit. (Hebrew *"mirmah"*, Strong's #4820)

Q: How does the concluding thought contrast to the treachery of the wicked?
> A: *"The sum of Your word is truth"* accepts God's Word as absolute even in spite of the personal circumstances, and *"…every one of Your righteous ordinances is everlasting"* is a way of stating that in spite of the temporal situation, the result is unalterably permanent when in compliance with God's Word.

Application: *While we are free to express our feelings, it cannot be automatically assumed that God will answer by altering or changing our emotions, which are subject to unpredictable shifts when His Word is not. As with most things in life, it is not a test of our feelings but a test of faith, especially when it comes to trusting God's already provided Word.*

Overall Application

Q: What do these teachings have in common?
A: They are very personal appeals to address very intense, personal issues.

Q: What is common to each which is diametrically opposite of the world's wisdom in such situations where we are personally concerned?
A: Whereas all worldly approaches advocate some kind of remedy to make us feel good as quick as possible, God's way is to continue in trust and obedience to His Word in spite of our emotions, even if they don't immediately change.

Q: What is common to most false teachings which reveals their design to undermine God's Word in our life?
A: They attempt to get us to fixate on this life at the expense of the next.

<u>Application:</u> Even when we go to Christ in times of the worst emotional despair, we still need to do so in combination with His Word.

Overall Application

Q: What is the difference between "reading" and "meditating"?
A: "Reading" is an informational approach, but "meditating" is incarnational—that is, the process by which God's Word becomes a part of us.

Q: How might that be important when it comes the working of the Word as our light?
A: Whereas an informational approach may show something about God's path, when the Word becomes a part of us we do not allow ourselves to stray from the path—we follow up with obedience.

Q: How might these teachings actually successively lead into each other?

- We incorporate God's Word into our prayer life.
- God's Word illuminates our way.
- God's Word works in us personally and as a visible witness.

Psalm 119 • Master for Handout (#19-20)

1. (v.145-152) **Qoph (ק): In the Meantime.** What is the correct response to every earthly situation where **God's Word** is concerned? Trust in **God's Word**.

2. (v.153-160) **Resh (ר): Revive Me.** While we are free to express our **feelings**, it cannot be automatically assumed that God will answer by altering or changing our *emotions*, which are subject to unpredictable **shifts** when His Word is not. As with most things in life, it is not a test of our **feelings** but a test of **faith**, especially when it comes to **trusting** God's already provided Word.

For Small Group Leaders to summarize these lessons:

Overall Application

Q: What do these teachings have in common?
   A: They are very personal appeals to address very intense, personal issues.

Q: What is common to each which is diametrically opposite of the world's wisdom in such situations where we are personally concerned?
   A: Whereas all worldly approaches advocate some kind of remedy to make us feel good as quick as possible, God's way is to continue in trust and obedience to His Word in spite of our emotions, even if they don't immediately change.

Q: What is common to most false teachings which reveals their design to undermine God's Word in our life?
   A: They attempt to get us to fixate on this life at the expense of the next.

Application: *Even when we go to Christ in times of the worst emotional **despair**, we still need to do so in **combination** with His Word.*

Psalm 119 Group Handout • Qoph & Resh (#19-20)

1. (v.145-152) **Qoph (ק): In the Meantime.** What is the correct response to every earthly situation where _____ is concerned? Trust in _____.

2. (v.153-160) **Resh (ר): Revive Me.** While we are free to express our _____, it cannot be automatically assumed that God will answer by altering or changing our _____, which are subject to unpredictable _____ when His Word is not. As with most things in life, it is not a test of our _____ but a test of _____, especially when it comes to _____ God's already provided Word.

Application: Even when we go to Christ in times of the worst emotional _____, we still need to do so in _____ with His Word.

Peter 14/2/22

Psalm 119:161-168, 169-176 • Shin & Tav (#21-22)

Introduction

[Note: Each stanza of Psalm 119 is a study in and of itself. For the purposes of leading a small group study, these three are presented together as a single study.]

It should not surprise anyone that Psalm 119 is the largest of the 929 chapters in our Bible as it is dedicated to not only explaining how Scripture is organized by its consistent use of 8 categories of God's Word, but repeatedly provides real world examples of how we are to apply every facet of God's Word to our life. The goal is not to determine what we can expect from God's Word, but that which we need to do to meet the personal shortfalls of what God's Word expects from us.

> ¹⁶¹Princes persecute me without cause,
> But my heart stands in awe of Your words.
> ¹⁶²I rejoice at Your word,
> As one who finds great spoil.
> ¹⁶³I hate and despise falsehood,
> But I love Your law.
> ¹⁶⁴Seven times a day I praise You,
> Because of Your righteous ordinances.
> ¹⁶⁵Those who love Your law have great peace,
> And nothing causes them to stumble.
> ¹⁶⁶I hope for Your salvation, O LORD,
> And do Your commandments.
> ¹⁶⁷My soul keeps Your testimonies,
> And I love them exceedingly.
> ¹⁶⁸I keep Your precepts and Your testimonies,
> For all my ways are before You.

[Read v.161-168] Love for Your Word

Q: How might the issue, "Princes persecute me without cause" (v.161) be associated to something relevant that we might experience in our own life?

A: This is easily substituted for governmental persecution and/or harassment.

Q: But like all the other types of opposition identified in Psalm 119 as originating with various types of human antagonists, how is the response still exactly the same as previously and repeatedly rendered?

A: "…but my heart stands in awe of Your words" (v.161) is exactly in line with every reaction to persecution, opposition and unfair treatment, to remain steadfast in obedience to God's Word and ways regardless.

Q: What is the main thought being conveyed where God's Word in general is concerned?

A: It is not just admiration for the Word or obedience out of fear, but a genuine love for it.

- (v.161) "…my heart stands in awe of Your words."
- (v.163) "…I love Your law."
- (v.167) "…I love them [Your testimonies] exceedingly."

117

Q: And what is the chief benefit listed of this deeper relationship with God's Word?

A: *"Those who love Your law have great peace, and nothing causes them to stumble".* (v.165)

Application: *It is not peace as the world defines it which obedience to God's Word and ways engenders, but the peace which comes to a believers who is living sin-free and in perfect character with His Word, what is here referred to as not stumbling.*

Q: What are the proper actions to be taken which are listed in v.166-168 undertaken by believers concerning God's Word?

- (v.166) *"I...do Your commandments."*
- (v.167) *"My soul keeps Your testimonies..."*
- (v.168) *"I keep Your precepts and Your testimonies..."*

Application: *How well do we recognize that biblical obedience is love-based? When we have an authentic relationship where we truly love someone, we have no issues of submission or compliance because incorporation of the rules is simply a pleasant part of that experience. We willfully limit our behavior.*

Q: What is significant about the closing confession, "For all my ways are before You"?

A: It is recognition that nothing is hidden from Christ.

Q: How does this fit in with the overall experience of love for His Word?

A: It is the conscience realization that there is no fear of everything being an open book to Christ when we are walking in accordance to His Word. His ways become our ways.

Application: *We need to recognize that our personal love for Christ must go hand-in-hand with our acknowledgment of the Apostle John's foundational teaching that Christ Himself is "the Word". (Jn. 1:1-5) We cannot love one with the other, which means not merely reading or listening to the Word, but becoming "an effectual doer". (Ja. 1:25) There is no authentic love relationship with Christ in the absence of complete obedience to His Word.*

*"You shall not worship them or serve them; for I, the LORD your God, am a jealous God, visiting the iniquity of the fathers on the children, on the third and the fourth generations of those who hate Me, but showing lovingkindness to thousands, **to those who love Me and keep My commandments**. — Exodus 20:5–6*

*"**If you love Me, you will keep My commandments**. — John 14:15*

*"**If you keep My commandments, you will abide in My love**; just as I have kept My Father's commandments and abide in His love. — John 15:10*

[Read v.169-179] The Word & Prayer

Q: Why might this closing section be surprising where the activity of prayer is concerned?

A: Although in each of the 22 instances the writer is obviously engaging in prayer, he rarely addresses the subject directly as provided here.

Q: Why do you suppose that is?

A: Because true, biblical faith is first and foremost grounded in obedience to God's Word and ways, for which no amount of prayer can act as a substitute.

Point: *A common false teaching is that "faith" is believing in something hard enough that God is moved to materialize it, especially in the areas of personal finances, health and worldly comfort. It is a false faith which is more akin to blowing out the candles on a birthday cake and wishing really hard for a pony. Biblically speaking, where there is no obedience to God's Word, for the believer there can be no authentic faith.*

> *So faith comes from hearing, and hearing by the word of Christ. (Romans 10:17)*

---

¹⁶⁹Let my cry come before You, O LORD;
Give me understanding according to Your word.
¹⁷⁰Let my supplication come before You;
Deliver me according to Your word.
¹⁷¹Let my lips utter praise,
For You teach me Your statutes.
¹⁷²Let my tongue sing of Your word,
For all Your commandments are righteousness.
¹⁷³Let Your hand be ready to help me,
For I have chosen Your precepts.
¹⁷⁴I long for Your salvation, O LORD,
And Your law is my delight.
¹⁷⁵Let my soul live that it may praise You,
And let Your ordinances help me.
¹⁷⁶I have gone astray like a lost sheep; seek Your servant,
For I do not forget Your commandments.

Q: What are the aspects of prayer which are presented here? And what is the requested response to each action?

- (v.169) *"Let my cry come before You..."* This is not a cry of desperation, but the Hebrew expression of rejoicing or making a joyful noise. The expected response is, *"Give me understanding according to Your word."*

- (v.170) *"Let my supplication come before You...:* A *"supplication"* is usually a request for mercy for oneself or others in the form of a prayer. The expected response is, *"Deliver me according to Your word."*

- (v.171) *"Let my lips utter praise..."* Biblical praise is completely devoted to the elevation of the character and working of God and completely devoid of any aspect of our self. The expected response is, *"...teach me Your statutes."*

- v.172) *"Let my tongue sing of Your word..."* This is describing one's testimony, not just making music. There is no expected response, but rather further personal affirmation, *"For all Your commandments are righteous."*

Point: *Notice how this is not some kind of "wish list" for something material or of benefit in this world, but approaching God in affirmation and praise of what His Word works in us.*

Application: *Because we most often employ prayer when things are wrong due to our own disobedience to God's Word, it is consumed with pleas for some kind of divine remedy. In this example, going to the Lord in a condition of obedience results in an overwhelming attitude of praise and thanksgiving.*

Q: What is the actual list of requested actions being submitted?

- (v.173) *"Let Your hand be ready to help me..."*
- (v.175) *"Let my soul live that it may praise You..."*
- (v.176) *"...seek Your servant..."*

Q: What is the reciprocal response on behalf of the believer for these things?

- (v.173) "...I have chosen Your precepts."
- (v.174) "...Your law is my delight."
- (v.175) "...let Your ordinances help me."
- (v.176) "...I do not forget Your commandments."

Application: *A prayer life which fails to not merely incorporate God's Word, but falls short of seeking an even greater personal commitment to it, is at best marginal. Such reveals both a wrong set of priorities and a shortfall where pursuing a deeper relationship where Christ is concerned.*

Overall Application

Q: How might these final two teachings summarize the most important themes of Psalm 119?
A: For those who actually and consistently put God's Word into practice, they don't simply admire or revere it, but come to love it; it therefore becomes an essential part of one's prayer life.

Q: What is the advantage enjoyed by those who truly love God's Word?
A: Because they are faithful to it regardless of the circumstances, their prayer life will be in alignment with God's will. Their love for and relationship with Christ will be in complete alignment with the Truth.

Application: *What does this say about someone who claims to love Jesus but rarely if ever reads, much less studies, their Bible? To what degree are your prayers formed around the truth of God's Word? If, as John states, Jesus IS "the Word", why don't we approach and observe it as if we are in His very presence?*

Psalm 119 • Handout for Master (#21-22)

1. (v.161-168) **Shin (ש): Love for Your Word.** We need to recognize that our personal **love** for Christ must go hand-in-hand with our acknowledgment of the Apostle John's foundational teaching that Christ Himself is **"the Word"**. (Jn. 1:1-5) We cannot **love** one with the other, which means not merely reading or listening to the Word, but becoming "an effectual **doer**". (Ja. 1:25) There is no authentic **love** relationship with Christ in the absence of complete **obedience** to His Word.

    *Application: What does this say about someone who claims to love Jesus but rarely if ever **reads**, much less **studies**, their Bible? To what degree are your prayers **formed** around the truth of God's Word? If, as John states, Jesus **IS** "the Word", why don't we **approach** and **observe** it as if we are in His very presence?*

2. (v.169-176) **Tav (ת): The Word & Prayer.** A prayer life which **fails** to not merely incorporate God's Word, but **falls short** of seeking an even greater personal commitment to it, is at best **marginal**. Such reveals both a wrong set of **priorities** and a **shortfall** where pursuing a deeper relationship where Christ is concerned.

For Small Group Leaders to summarize these three lessons:

Overall Application

Q: How might these final two teachings summarize the most important themes of Psalm 119?

A: For those who actually and consistently put God's Word into practice, they don't simply admire or revere it, but come to love it; it therefore becomes an essential part of one's prayer life.

Q: What is the advantage enjoyed by those who truly love God's Word?

A: Because they are faithful to it regardless of the circumstances, their prayer life will be in alignment with God's will. Their love for and relationship with Christ will be in complete alignment with the Truth.

Psalm 119 Group Handout • Shin & Tav (#21-22)

1. **(v.161-168) Shin (ש): Love for Your Word.** We need to recognize that our personal _____ for Christ must go hand-in-hand with our acknowledgment of the Apostle John's foundational teaching that Christ Himself is "_____". (Jn. 1:1-5) We cannot _____ one with the other, which means not merely reading or listening to the Word, but becoming "an effectual _____". (Ja. 1:25) There is no authentic _____ relationship with Christ in the absence of complete _____ to His Word.

2. **(v.169-176) Tav (ת): The Word & Prayer.** A prayer life which _____ to not merely incorporate God's Word, but _____ of seeking an even greater personal commitment to it, is at best _____. Such reveals both a wrong set of _____ and a _____ where pursuing a deeper relationship where Christ is concerned.

Application: *What does this say about someone who claims to love Jesus but rarely if ever _____, much less _____ their Bible? To what degree are your prayers _____ around the truth of God's Word? If, as John states, Jesus IS "the Word", why don't we _____ it as if we are in His very presence?*

123

Notes:

Printed in Great Britain
by Amazon